THE CENTRAL
CONCEPTION OF BUDDHISM

AND THE
MEANING OF THE WORD "DHARMA"

By
TH STCHERBATSKY

★

INDOLOGICAL BOOK HOUSE
Delhi. 1970 Varanasi.

FIRST EDITION, LONDON, 1923
SECOND EDITION, CALCUTTA, 1956
THIRD EDITION, CALCUTTA, 1961
FOURTH EDITION, DELHI, 1970

Rs. 10/-

Published by Shri Bhagwan Singh, Indological Book House,
CK 31/10 Nipali Khapra, Varanasi & Printed at Liberty Art Press,
Daryaganj, Delhi by Offset Process,

CONTENTS

PREFACE

This short treatise was originally conceived as a contribution to the Royal Asiatic Society's *Journal*: its size induced the Council to publish it as a monograph, and my best thanks are due to the Council for this kind decision. I must also express my gratitude to Mrs. C. A. F. Rhys Davids, who was always ready to help with her vast knowledge of Pali literature. Professor H. Jacobi kindly went through the proofs, and to him I am indebted for many a valuable suggestion. Dr. McGovern contributed some of the references to Chinese sources. But my deepest gratitude is due to Dr. F. W. Thomas, who devoted much of his precious time to the revision of my work and to carrying it through the press.

In transliteration I have usually not distinguished the guttural etc. nasals, when occurring before the consonants of their respective classes.

July, 1923.   TH. STCHERBATSKY

CORRIGENDA

P. 1. n. 2. line 13 for p. 323 read 823.

P. 7-8. The *ayatanas* 1-6 to be treated as internal bases (*adhyatma-ayatana*) and 7-12 as external bases (*bahya-ayatana*)

P. 13. n. 43, treat the line 5 as line 4.

P. 14. n. 44. line 1 after op. cit put pp. 68-69.

P. 14. n. 44. line 7 for p. 81 read pp. 70-71.

P. 16. line 3 for *latter* read *later*.

1. PRELIMINARY

In a recent work* Mrs. M. Geiger and Professor W. Geiger have made an attempt to solve the uncertainty which still prevails about the meaning of the term *dharma*.[1] They have drawn up a concordance of almost every case where the word occurs in Pali canonical literature, and established a great variety of meanings. Among them there is, indeed, only one that really matters, that is the specifically Buddhistic technical term *dharma*. The other significations which Buddhist literature shares with the Brahmanical do not present any serious difficulty. About this meaning the authors rightly remark that it is a "central conception of the Buddhist doctrine which must be elucidated as far as possible." They also contend that the method followed by them is "purely philological." This is also an indication of the limitations of their work, because the central conception of a highly complicated system, a conception which in its varied connotations includes almost the totality of the system, cannot be expected to be fully elucidated by "philological" methods only. We therefore propose, in addition to Mrs. and Professor Geiger's most valuable collections, to consider the matter from the philosophical standpoint, *i.e.*, to give, with regard to this conception, a succint account of the system in which it admittedly occupies the keystone position. Our chief source will be, not the Pali Canon, but a later work, the *Abhidhammakoca* of Vasubandhu.[2] Although late, it is pro

---

* A.D. 1925 in which year the first edition of this book was published.

[1] *Pali Dhamma*, von Magdalene u. Wilhelm Geiger, Munich, 1921.

[2] A plan of an edition and translation of the whole work has been outlined and partly carried through by the *Bibliotheca Buddhica* at Petrograd. There have appeared, (1) *Abhidharma-koca-karika* and *Bhasya*, Tibetan text, pt. i. edited by Professor Th. Stcherbatsky. Petrograd, 1917; (2) *Sphutarthabhidharma-koca-vyakhya* of Yasomitra. Sanscrit text. pt. 1, edited by S. Levi and Th. Stcherbatsky, Petrograd, 1917. The second parts of both these works, Tibetan text edition by Professor Th. Stcherbatsky and Vyakhya (Sanscrit) by Professor W. Wogihara of Tokyo, are being printed in the *Bibliotheca Buddhica*. An English translation of the ninth (additional) part has been published by Professor Th. Stcherbatsky under the title "The Soul Theory of the Buddhists" in the *Bulletin de l'Academie des Sciences de Russie*, Petrograd, 1920 (pp. 323-54 and 937-58). A review of the system has been published by the late Professor O. Rosenberg, of Petrograd University, under the title *Problems of Buddhist Philosophy*, Petrograd, 1918 (in

fessedly only a systematized exposition of a much earlier work—the *Adhidharma-vibhasa-sastra,* which, in its turn, is but a commentary on the *abhidharma* of the Sarvastivadin school. This school is one of the earliest, if not the earliest, of Buddhist sects. The question upon which it dissented and from which it received its name had a bearing on the essence of what was called a *dharma,* so that an exposition of its views will afford the best opportunity of examining the full connotation of this term.[3] It must be left to later investigation to determine the points where Vasubandhu's exposition may be at variance with the primitive doctrine; but, generally speaking, he seems to have rendered the original doctrine very faithfully. Since his age is about the same as that of the Pali commentaries,[4] the difference between him and the Pali sources is not so much one of time as of school. Nothing is more instructive than the study of the divergent views of different schools, since it allows us to watch the builders of the Buddhist doctrine at work.

The formula of the Buddhist Credo (*ye dhamma,* etc.)—which professedly contains the shortest statement of the essence and the spirit of Buddhism[5]—declares that Buddha discovered the elements (*dhamma*) of existence, their causal connexion, and a method to suppress their efficiency for ever

Russian). This scholar has also issued an index of Buddhist technical terms in Chinese and Japanese under the title *An Introduction to the study of Buddhism from Chinese and Japanese Sources,* Tokyo, 1917. Professor de la Vallee Poussin has published in Brussels a French translation of the third part, and is now engaged in printing a translation of the first and second parts of the *Abhidharma-kosa.*

[3] Beside Mrs. and Prof. Geiger the question has been treated by Mrs. Rhys Davids, *Bud. Psy. Ethics,* xxxiii; Walleser, *Grundlage,* 97-104; Warren, *Buddhism in Translation,* 116-209 ; S. Z. Aung, *Compendium,* 179 n., 254-9; S. Levi, *Sutralamkara,* 18, 21; L. de la Vallee Poussin, *Notes sur les corps du Bouddha,* Museon, 1913, pp. 263, 287. The question has been put in the proper light and brilliantly treated by Professor O. Rosenberg, *Problems,* chap. vi ; but, since his work is written in Russian and inaccessible at present, some of his results are repeated here.

[4] The date of Vasubandhu is not yet quite settled ; cf. the references in V. Smith, *Early History,* 3rd ed., pp. 328 ff. At the end of chap. viii Vasubandhu remarks that in his time the *agama* had had an existence of 1,000 (not 900) years, and the *adhigama* (=*abhidharma*) somewhat less than that. That there were two Vasubandhus is not "a guess with no solid basis"; the Kosa actually quotes the opinions of a *vriddhacharya* Vasubandhu and rejects them (i. 13, Tibetan text, p. 23; cf. Yasomitra's comment). There remain the dates of the Chinese translations of the works of Asanga and Vasubandhu, which alone, if correct, would be sufficient evidence to assign them to the fourth century. Otherwise one feels inclined to bring Vasubandhu nearer to Dignaga, whose teacher he was.

[5] Cf. *Mahavagga,* i. 23.

(*nirodha*). Vasubandhu makes a similar statement about the essence of the doctrine: it is a method of converting the elements of existence into a condition of rest, out of which they never will emerge again.[6] From the first days of the Buddhist church the novices, before obtaining admittance into the order, went through a course of instruction in what may be termed the Buddhist catechism, *i.e.*, an exposition of the elements (*dharma*) of existence and their different classifications into *skandhas, ayatanas, dhatus*.[7] The same training was considered indispensable for the aspiring nuns.[8] These conditions have not changed down to the present day in all Buddhist countries. In the whole of Mongolia and Tibet, in those parts of Siberia where Buddhism is spreading against the primitive Shamanism among the Tunguz tribes of Transbaikalia, in the governments of Irkutsk and Astrachan, where it is maintaining itself against orthodox Christianity—everywhere it invariably proceeds by starting religious schools (*chos-grva*), where manuals similar to the *Dhamma-samgani* containing tables of *dharmas* are carefully studied, in the Tibetan original with explanations in vernacular, by the young generation aspiring to be admitted to the order and to be gradually promoted to the higher ecclesiastical ranks. Scholars of Buddhism in Europe will do well to follow this example.

A school of Buddhists which claims as its fundamental doctrine the principle that "everything exists" has very naturally been supposed to uphold some kind of realistic views.[9] Tradition affirms that the question which gave rise to this sect had been discussed at the time of Buddha himself. If a division arises in a community with the result that some of its members are declared to be, or claim to be, realists, one

---

[6] *Ab. K.*, i., 1, Tib. text, p. 3, 11, 12-13.

[7] Cf. *Theragatha*, 1255 :
  *tassaham vacanam sutva khandhe ayatanani ca
  dhatuyo ca viditvana pabbajim anagariyam.*

[8] Cf. Geiger's references to *Therigathas*, op. cit., p. 65; the *dhatus* there mentioned are probably the eighteen *dhatus* (not the six); a number of other divisions into *dhatus* are mentioned in the *Bahu-dhatuka-sutra*, cf. *Ab. K.*, i., 27, Tib. text, p. 46.

[9] So Takakusu s.v. in *Hastings' Encyclopædia*. S. Z. Aung and Mrs. C. Rhys Davids, *Points of Controversy*, pp. 275-6, rightly observe that the question bears upon the existence of future and past *dharmas*, but this does not mean that "they believed in continued or immutable existence of everything." This would be drifting into Sankhya doctrine, against which Buddhist philosophers were always uttering warnings; cf. Appendix I.

would naturally be led to suppose that there were others who were non-realists, *i.e.*, idealists of some kind. But, as a matter of fact, we do not meet with views definitely idealistic, *i.e.*, with the denial of the existence of external objects, until a comparatively late date. Considering, on the other hand, that these would-be realists, like all Buddhists, denied the existence of a soul or a personality (*atman, pudgala*), our uncertainty increases, and the suspicion arises that the battle between the Sarvastivadins and their opponents was fought on an altogether different plane, about a question which had little to do with our conceptions of realism and idealism.[10]

The occasion upon which Buddha himself is supposed to have put forward the watchword "everything exists" was a discussion with the Ajivikas, who flatly denied the influence of past deeds upon our destinies, since they were past and non-existent.[11] This sect upheld a kind of extreme determinism which served as excuse for moral incontinence; it maintained that "all things are inalterably fixed. There is no cause, either proximate or remote, for the depravity of being, or... for its purity... There is no such thing as power or energy or human exertion. Everything that thinks, has senses, is procreated, and lives, is destitute of force, power or energy. Their varying conditions, at any time, are due to fate, to their environment and their own nature."[12] Buddha's teaching, both in the moral domain and in ontology, was the reverse of this; it maintained moral responsibility and at the same time transformed all existing things into a congeries of subtle energies (*samskara-samuha*). When pressed to say what was meant by the words "everything exists," he answered "everything exists means that the twelve *ayatanas* exist."[13] Now the

[10] The Buddhists themselves ascribe the origin of their idealistic philosophy to Vasubandhu; cf. my article in the Museon, 1905, ii. But this was evidently only a revival of a tendency which, in a different form, was already revealed in the works of Asvaghosa and Nagarjuna. *Ab. K.* bears witness that idealistic views were already discussed in the *Vibhasa-sastra*; cf. i. 42. Tibetan text, p. 77, 10, and Yashomitra's comment.

[11] *Ab. K.* ad. v. 24; cf. Appendix 1.

[12] Cf. R. Hoernle's article in *Hastings' Encyclopædia*.

[13] This passage (*Samyuktagama*, xiii. p. 16 (McGovern) cannot be traced in the Pali Canon. Evidently the Theravadins suppressed it because it did not agree with their particular tenets. They accused the Vatsiputriyas of having suppressed the passages which ran against their views (*Soul Theory*, p. 840), and evidently did themselves the same. But even in their school the word *sabba* seems to have been used rather like a technical term. It did not mean "everything," but every item of the Buddhist table of elements. This table was supposed to be an "exhaus-

twelve *ayatanas* are merely one of the many classifications of the elements of existence of matter and mind. The Sarvastivadin school admitted seventy-five such elements. These elements were called *dharmas*. The full meaning of the term will emerge at the end of this article; at present we take it to mean an ultimate entity, the conception of which in the domain of matter, excludes the reality of everything except sense-data, and in the field of mind, of everything except separate mental phenomena. We will begin by reviewing the different kinds of elements and their various classifications, and then proceed to determine what was the Buddhist conception of an element of existence. This will lead us to ascertain more precisely in what sense the older Buddhist doctrine may have a claim to be called a realistic system.

II. SKANDHAS

The simplest classification of all elements of existence is represented by a division into five groups of elements: (1) matter, (2) feelings, (3) ideas, (4) volitions and other faculties, and (5) pure sensation or general consciousness.[14] If we realize that the group of matter represents no other matter than sense-data, that a soul is excluded and replaced by feelings, ideas, volitions and pure sensation, we cannot but be surprised that from under a cover of Oriental terminology an epitome of matter and mind emerges which very nearly approaches the standpoint of modern European science.

Three of these groups, namely, feelings, ideas, and pure sensation, contain one element (*dharma*) each. They are, nevertheless, called groups because they include feelings, etc., as past, present, and future, proximate and remote, external and internal, morally pure or impure, etc.[15] The group of matter includes ten elements, ten different varieties of sense-data.[16] The group of volitions, etc., includes fifty-eight elements, various mental faculties and general forces.[17]

---

tive division" : cf. Mrs. Rhys Davids, *Buddhist Psychology*, p. 41 ; *Samyutta*, iv. 15-27 : *Visuddhi-Magga*, ch. xiv : Warren, *Buddhism in translation*, p. 158; G. Grimm. *Buddhismus, passim*.

[14] The reasons for these renderings of the terms *rupa*, *vedana*, *samjna*, *samskara*, and *vijnana* will be given later on.

[15] *Ab. K.*, i. 20.

[16] Ibid., i, 14.

[17] All the *samskaras* except *vedana* and *samjna*, ibid., i, 15. The three eternal elements—*asamskrta*—are not included in the *skandhas* ibid., i, 22. Together with *arijnapti-rupa* this will make seventy-five elements in all.

The physical elements of a personality, including its outer world—the external objects—are represented in this classification by one item—matter;[18] the mental ones are distributed among the four others.

For "Matter and Mind" the old pre-Buddhistic term *nama-rupa* is used, where *rupa* represents the elements of matter and *nama* includes the four mental classes.

But the most general division of all elements is into matter (*rupa*), mind (*citta-caitta*), and forces (*samskara*). The fourth group (*samskara-skandha*), which includes mental faculties and general forces, is here split into two parts; the mental faculties are then united to all other mental groups, and are brought under the head of mind; the general forces or energies receive a separate place (*citta-viprayukta-samskara*).[19] This threefold division is very popular and known in Mongolia and Tibet to every schoolboy.[20]

III. AYATANAS

A second, more detailed, classification of the elements is made with a view to a division into cognitive faculties and their objects. There are six cognitive faculties and six categories of corresponding objects. They make the twelve *ayatanas* or "bases" of cognition, viz.:

    I. Six internal bases (*adhyatma-ayatana*) or respective faculties (*indriya*).

   II. Six external bases (*bahyaayatana*) or objects (*visaya*).

    1. Sense of vision (*caksur-endriya-ayatana*).

    2. Sense of audition (*crotr-endriya-ayatana*).

    3. Sense of smelling (*ghran-endriya-ayatana*).

    4. Sense of taste (*jihv-endriya-ayatana*).

    5. Sense of touch (*kay-endriya-ayatana*).

    6. Faculty of the intellect or consciousness (*mana-indriya-ayatana*).

    7. Colour and shape (*rupa-ayatana*).

---

[18] Among the physical elements there is one called *avijnapti* which broadly corresponds to what we might call the moral character of a person; for some special reasons it is entered by the Sarvastivadins in their physical class (*rupa*), but other schools include it in mind (*Ab. K.*, i, 11). In the *ayatana* and *dhatu* classifications it is included not in the physical items, but in the general class *dharmah*, i.e. *ayatana* or *dhatu* No. 12. In the following account we leave this special element unnoticed, cf. Appendix II, under *Matter*.

[19] Or a slightly differing fivefold division : *rupa, citta, caitta, viprayukta-samskara*, and *nirvana*; cf. *Ab. K.*, ii, 22, and Appendix II.

[20] *Zuge-ces-Idan-min-hdu-byed.*

8.   Sound (*sabda-ayatana*).
9.   Odour (*gandha-ayatana*).
10. Taste (*rasa-ayatana*).
11. Tangible (*sprastavya-ayatana*).
12. Non-sensuous objects (*dharma-ayatana* or *dharmah*).

In this classification the eleven first items correspond to eleven elements (*dharma*), each including one. The twelfth item contains all the remaining sixty-four elements, and it is therefore called *dharma-ayatana* or simply *dharmah, i.e.,* the *remaining* elements.

The term *ayatana* means "entrance" (*ayam tanoti*). It is an "entrance" for consciousness and mental phenomena (*citta-caittanam*). Consciousness, it is stated, never arises alone, since it is pure sensation, without any content. It is always supported or "introduced" by two elements: a cognitive faculty and a corresponding objective element. These are the supporters or the "doors" (*dvara*) for consciousness to appear. Visual consciousness (*caksur-vijnana*) arises in correlation (*pratitya*) with the sense of vision (*caksur-indriya*) and some colour (*rupam ca*). In the case of the sixth cognitive faculty (*manas*), consciousness itself, *i.e.,* its preceding moment, acts as a faculty for apprehending non-sensuous objects.

The trend of this classification, which is a characteristic feature of Buddhism from its very beginnings, is unmistakable. It intends to give a division of all objects of cognition into sense-objects and nonsensuous ones. The first are then divided into ten groups according to the five senses and their five objects, and the second (*dharma-ayatana,* or simply *dharmah*), including every nonsensuous object, is left undivided. There are six items corresponding to six cognitive faculties. Thus the twelve *ayatanas,* or "bases of cognition," represent all elements of existence distributed within six subjective and six corresponding objective items. Their synonym is "everything" (*sarvam*). When the principle "everything exists" is set forth it has the meaning that nothing but the twelve bases of cognition are existent. An object which cannot be viewed as a *separate* object of cognition or a *separate* faculty of cognition is unreal, as *e.g..* the soul, or the personality. Being a congeries of separate elements it is declared to be a name, and not a reality, not a *dharma* [21]

[21] The right explanation of the term *ayatana* is given in O. Rosenberg's *Problems.* p. 138 ff. The usual translation "sphere" ignores the

IV. DHATUS

The division of the elements of existence into eighteen *dhatus*, although very similar—it represents, indeed, in its first twelve items a repetition of the former one—is taken from a quite different view-point. Buddhist philosophy is an analysis of separate elements, or forces, which unite in the production of one stream (*samtana*) of events. The unphilosophic mind of common people supposes this stream to represent a personality or an individual (*pudgala*). Viewed as components of such a stream the elements are called *dhatus*. Just as different metals (*dhatus*) might be extracted out of a mine, just so does the stream of an individual life reveal elements of eighteen different kinds (*dhatu=gotra*).[22] It always includes six faculties (from *caksur-dhatu* up to *mano-dhatu*), six kinds of objective elements (from *rupa-dhatu* up to *dharma-dhatu*), and six kinds of consciousness, beginning with visual consciousness, or visual sensation (*caksur-vijnana-dhatu*), and ending with consciousness purely mental, i.e., non-sensuous (*mano-vijnana-dhatu*). Thus, in addition to the twelve components corresponding to the twelve bases of cognition, we have:

13. Visual consciousness   (*caksur-vijnana-dhatu*).
14. Auditory   „   (*srotra-vijnana-dhatu*).
15. Olfactory   „   (*ghrana-vijnana-dhatu*).
16. Gustatory   „   (*jihva-vijnana-dhatu*).
17. Tactile   „   (*kaya-vijnana-dhatu*).
18. Non-sensuous „   (*mano-vajnana-dhatu*).

Consciousness, which is but one element (*dharma*), is split in this classification into seven items, since it enters into the composition of an individual life as a faculty (*mano-dhatu*) and as six different kinds of sensations, differentiated by their origin, as from one of the senses, or from a purely mental non-sensuous source.[23]

fundamentum divisionis. S. Z. Aung, *Compendium*, p. 256, although containing the right suggestion, thinks it "might well be left untranslated."

[22] *Ab. K.*, i., 20. It may be noted that the number of component elements (*tattvas*) of the rudimentary body in Sankhya is likewise eighteen. That the term *dhatu* has been borrowed from medical science where it means element of the body, can hardly be doubted.

[23] *Dhatu* is often defined just as *dharma* : *sva-svabhava-dharanat*, or *sva-laksana-dharanat* (cf. S. Z. Aung. *Compendium*, P. 255ff). But this is only partly correct, since the *dhatu* No. 12 includes sixty-four *dharmas*, and the seven *dhatus*. No. 6 and Nos. 13-18, correspond to

All these varieties of consciousness exist only in the ordinary plane of existence (kama-Dhatu). In higher worlds (rupa-Dhatu) sense consciousness gradually disappears, in the immaterial worlds (arupa-Dhatu) only non-sensuous consciousness is left. A division of consciousness into various kinds (dhatu 13-18) is thus made necessary for the composition of formulas of elements corresponding to the denizens of various worlds.[24]

We will now proceed to consider the separate elements in the order of their most general classification into Matter, Mind, and Forces.

V. ELEMENTS OF MATTER

Matter (rupa) or the physical elements (rupino, dharmah), which in the first classification occupied one item (rupa-skandha), is otherwise distributed into ten items (Nos. 1-5 and 7-11). The term rupa-ayatana is reserved for visible matter or, more precisely, the phenomenon of visibility alone, this being matter par excellence.[25] The general characteristic of matter, or material elements, is impenetrability (sa-pratighatva), which is defined as the fact that space occupied by one of them cannot, at the same time, be occupied by another.[26]

one single dharma—the vijnana (=manas=cittam). The definition in Ab. K. i., 20, is dhatu=gotra. We can, accordingly, translate dhatu by "component," "element," or "class of elements," just as the case may require.

[24] When the three Dhatus are mentioned the term Dhatu means world (loka) or plane of existence (avacara). It has nothing to do with the eighteen dhatus. The worlds are divided into material (rupa-) and immaterial (arupa-) worlds, the former again into worlds of carnal desire or defiled matter—kama-(rupa)-Dhatu, and those of pure, or reduced, matter—(niskama-) rupa-Dhatu. In the kama-Dhatu life consists of eighteen components (dhatus), in the rupa-Dhatu of fourteen (excepted are Nos. 9-10 and 15-16), in the arupa-Dhatu of three (Nos. 6, 12, and 18). In rupa- and arupa-Dhatus life is characterized by different degrees of perpetual trance (dhyana). Ordinary people can be transferred into these higher regions of trance either through being reborn in them ((utpatti) or through an effort of transic meditation (samapatti).

[25] Ab. K., i. 24.

[26] The etymological explanation is: rupyata iti rupam, i.e., matt is what materializes. Different meanings are then given of this mater lizing: pressure, pain, disappearance, or change. Thus matter is something that disappears. The real meaning is impenetrability (sa-pratig-hatva), which is further variously explained. Kumaralabha gives to the phenomenon of impenetrability an idealistic interpretation: "the impossibility for the intellect to imagine the presence of two such objects occupying the same space." (ibid. Tibetan text, p. 50, 17 ff). O. Rosenberg strongly objects to the interpretation of rupa as matter. He maintains that Buddhism from its very outset viewed the phenomenal world as an illusion and relegated every reality to some transcendental world (cf. Problems, chap. x). He suggests 'sense-elements" for rupa. This

The elements of visibility are divided into two main groups, colours and shapes. There are eight colours and twelve different shapes. Another theory reduces all colours to two, light and darkness. All other varieties of visibility are represented as differences of lines. The opposite view, namely, that colours alone are realities and shapes (*samsthana*) represent constructions of the mind (*manasam, parikalpitam*), (superimposed upon the difference of coloration as an interpretation of it), was favoured by the Sautrantikas.[27]   A line, say a line drawn by the motion of the hand; being an intimation of something (*vijnapti*) is an element (*rupa-dharma*) of length[28]; the line of the flight of a bird in the air is the same. They are interpreted as the apparitions of the element of length of some colour and all Buddhist matter must be conceived according to this pattern. They are material elements without any matter in them.

A glance at the ten items corresponding to matter in the *ayatana*-division will convince us that no other matter except sense-data is recognized. It is broadly divided into two categories, objective sense-data (*visaya*) constituting external objects, and sense-organs (*indriya*) conceived as a kind of translucent subtle *matter* which covers the body when it is living. This division reminds us of the Sankhya view that matter developed along two different lines, the one with predominance of the translucent intelligence-stuff (*sattva*) resulting in sense-organs, the other, with predominance of dead matter (*tamas*), resulting in sense-objects in their subtle (*tanmatra*) and gross (*mahabhuta*) forms. In fact the concept of *tan-matra* comes very near to the Buddhist conception of an element of matter (*rupa-dharma*). The fundamental difference between the two conceptions is that in the Sankhya system these elements are modifications or appurtenances of an eternal substance. In Buddhism they are mere sense-data without any substance.

The translucent matter of the sense-organs (*rupa-prasada*) is very subtle; it is like the shining of a jewel, it cannot be

would find a place in an idealistic system and would be supported by the above interpretation of Kumaralabha. But it is, evidently, not the view adopted by the school of the Sarvastivadins. It is true that there is no other matter than sense-data. This should not prevent us, just as it does not prevent modern philosophers who favour the same view, from using the term "matter" for facts characterized by impenetrability.

[27] *Ab. K.*, i, 10, and Yac. comment.

[28] *Ab. K.*, i, 10, Tib. text, p. 17.

cut in two,[29] it cannot be burnt,[30] it has no weight,[31] and it disappears without a residue at death.[32] It is nevertheless, atomic, and is represented by five different kinds of atoms. The atoms of the organ of sight (caksur-indriya) cover in concentric circles the eye-ball. The atoms of the organ of taste, or, more precisely, that matter which is supposed to convey the sensation of taste, covers in concentric semicircles the tongue. The atoms of the organs of touch (kay-endriya) cover the whole body.[33] The idea that all these different kinds of special matter are, indeed, the same translucent subtle stuff covering the whole living body and disappearing at death had also its advocates, who consequently reduced all senses to one, the sense of touch, but this did not find general acceptance. Being as subtle as the shining of a jewel, this matter cannot appear alone; it is supported by gross matter (mahabhuta), of which the eye-ball and flesh in general consist.

The atoms of external matter are likewise divided into atoms of general, universal, or fundamental matter, and special atoms of colour-, sound-, tangibility-matter, etc. The fundamental elements are four in number; they are manifested by the facts of hardness or repulsion, cohesion or attraction, heat and motion.[34] Conventionally they are called earth, water, fire, and air; but it is specified that these are only conventional appellations, and that in the name of the fourth general element (irana) alone both the technical and the usual meanings coalesce, because the word irana has both the significations of motion and air as well.[35] The fact that the fourth element is motion is an indication of the trend of this division; the general elements of matter, like all Buddhist elements, are more forces than substances. These four elements appear always together, always in equal proportion. There is as much element of heat in a blazing flame as there is in wood

---

[29] If a member, or all members, are chopped off the body, the sense-organ matter is not cut even in two parts, i.e., the parts that are cut off are senseless. The movements of a lizard's tale after it is knocked off the main body are explained by the presence of this life-matter (indriya), but by the intensification of the rayu element, i.e., it is a lifeless process (Ab. K., i, 36, Tibetan text, p. 63, and Yash. comment).

[30] Ab. K., i, 36, Tib. text, p. 63, 13.

[31] Ibid.

[32] Ab. K., i., 37. and Yac. comment: mrtasya ananuvrttch. This is a point of analogy with the linga-sarira of the Sankhyas.

[33] Ab. K., i. 44, Tibetan text, p. 84, 15 ff.

[34] Ab. K., i. 12.

[35] Ab. K., i. 13.

or in water, and vice versa, the difference is only in their intensity.[36] The general elements of matter (mahabhuta) are
brought under the head of tangibles (ayatana No. 11). Since
there is only a limited number of general manifestations of
tangibility, therefore their number is four.[37] There is,
apparently, a distinction between the elements in themselves
and their manifestations, because the four facts of resistance,
attraction, heat, and motion are clearly called manifestations
(laksana) of the elements (dharma), which, accordingly
must be something different, something mysterious or transcendental, similar in this respect to the gunas of the Sankhyas.
The other five kinds of objective matter (ayatanas Nos. 7-11)
were not general, but special, corresponding to each of the
five senses; the tangibility-matter alone (ayatana No. 11) includes both the general (mahabhuta) and the special (Bhautika) elements of matter.[38] They were also atomic but could
not appear independently without being combined with the
fundamental ones, in the ratio of four atoms of primary matter to one of secondary. Thus the minimum number of
atoms indispensable for their actual appearance in life was
eight: four atoms of general materiality combined with each
atom of colour, odour, taste, and secondary tangibility-
matter (such as smoothness, coarseness, etc.). If the particular piece of matter resounded, atoms of sound were added and
the combination consisted then of nine different atoms.[39] The
combined atoms (sanghata-paramanu) alone appear in phenomenal reality; the simple ones, or infra-atomic elements,
presumably, were relegated to transcendental reality, in accordance with the general character of a Buddhist element.
This device made it an easy task for Buddhists to oppose the
indivisibility of atoms.[40]

[36] e.g., the tactile sensation may have a different degree of intensity
as the touch by a bunch of steel needles is more intensely felt than the
touch of a painter's brush, although the quantity may be the same. The
existence of cohesiveness, i.e., of the element "water" in a flame, is
proved by its keeping a shape; the presence of repulsion, i.e., of the
element "earth", in water is proved by the fact of its supporting a ship,
etc. (cf. Ab. K., ii, 22, and Yashom).

[37] Ab. K., i. 35, Tibetan text, p. 61, 5 ff.

[38] Ibid.

[39] The actual number of atoms in a sanghata-paramanu will be much
greater, since each atom of secondary (bhautika) matter needs a set of
four primary atoms of its own, but if dhatus alone are reckoned the
number will express the classes (dhatu) of elements (dharma) represented (cf. Ab. K., ii, 22).

[40] Ab. K., i., 43, Tibetan text, p. 83.

VI. ELEMENTS OF MIND

In the *ayatana* classification two items (Nos. 6 and 12) are devoted to the elements of mind (*citta-caitta-dharmah, arupino dharmah*) and, according to the principle of this classification, they represent two correlative groups; a subjective one (*indriya*) and an objective one (*visaya*). The principle of externality of one element in regard to another *i.e.*, the idea of separate elements (*prthag-dharma*) is maintained in the field of mind just as in the field of matter. Mind is split into two chief parts. The subjective part, or mind viewed as a receptive faculty, is represented by one element called, indiscriminately, *citta, vijnana,* or *manas.*[41] It represents pure consciousness, or pure sensation, without any content. Its content is placed in the objective part which contains the definite sensation (*sparsa*), feelings (*vedana*), ideas (*sanjna*), volitions (*cetana*), and various other mental phenomena up to the number of forty-six separate elements.[42] So it is that feelings come to be viewed as objects of the mind, a position which, for other reason they likewise possess in the Sankhya system. The category in which they are entered is called the (general) group of elements (*dharma-ayatana*) or simply "the elements" (*dharmah*). As stated above, the first eleven "bases" contain one element (*dharma*) each, but this last one contains the remaining sixty-four elements of the list. Beside the forty-six mental phenomena it contains the fourteen elementary forces (*viprayukta-samskara*), the element of character (*avijnapti*) and the three eternal elements (*asamskrta*): among the latter is Nirvana, the chief *dharma.* For this reason the term "elements" (*dharmah*) is a sufficient indication of this group, because the other categories, although also containing elements (*dharmah*), have a special name each.[43] The common feature of all these elements is that they are apprehended by the intellect directly without any intermediate agency of the

[41] *Ab. K.*, ii, 34. The same terms in the Pali Canon, *Samyutta*, ii, 94.
[42] The Theravada reckoned fifty-one. Cf. the fifty *bhavas* of the Sankhyas, some of them exhibiting an analogy with corresponding Buddhist *caitta-dharmas.* A full list of the forty-six *caitta-dharmas* is given below. App. II.
[43] Every *ayatana* is thus a *dharmayatana*, but No. 12 is *dharmayatana* par excellence. Just so is it that the ten material *ayatanas* all include matter. They are, consequently, all of them, *rupayatanas.* But *rupayatana* is its special designation, because it represents the most only one of them—the visible element ; *ayatana* No. 7—retains the name characteristic and important among the elements of matter. Cf. *Ab. K.* i, 24, Tibetan text, p. 42, 17 ff.

senses. In the apprehension of sense-objects there is likewise participation by the intellect; but these *dharmah* are non-sensuous objects, they are the exclusive domain of the receptive intellect, just as colour is the exclusive domain of he sense of vision.[44] The definition of receptive consciousness is pregnant: *vijnanam prativijnaptih*, *i.e.*, "consciousness is an intimation, or awareness, in every single case" (of what is now present to the senses, or to the mind directly).[45] If an apprehension contains some, albeit quite indefinite, content, say some indefinite visual sensation, it will then represent the next degree, a real sensation (*sparsa*).[46] The definite preception (*parichitti*) of a colour will be an "idea" (*sanjna*), but consciousness as the perceptive faculty is pure sensation. Although quite undifferentiated in itself, this pure sensation is, nevertheless, distinguished from the standpoint of its origin or, more precisely, its environment, *i.e.*, the elements by which its appearance is accompanied. From this point of view, as stated above, there is a set of six different kinds (*dhatu*) of consciousness, corresponding to a set of six receptive faculties and a set of six kinds of objects. We thus have six categories of consciousness (*sad-vijnana-kayah*), begining with visual sensation or, more precisely, pure sensation arising in connexion with some colour (*caksur-vijnana-dhatu*) and ending with consciousness accompanying a non-sensuous object (*mano-vijnana-dhatu*). We have besides the same consciousness as a receptive faculty (*dhatu* No. 6). As a receptive faculty *mano-dhatu* is not different from consciousness arising in connexion

---

[44] Prof. and Mrs. Geiger. op. cit., have established for the *dharmah* in the technical sense the signification "the empirical things." This is an example of the importance of the "philological method" ! It has not escaped their attention that *dharmah* is synonymous with *dharmayatana* and *dharmadhatu*, in which Nirvana is included (p. 83) which is anything but empirical. The *dharmah* are apprehended by *monah* (p. 81), but the emphasis is put on the fact that they are apprehended *without the co-operation of the senses*. Everything is apprehended by *monah*, but the *dharmah* are external with regard to *manah*; their place in the system is among the six *visaya*, as opposed to the six *indriya*, one of which, the sixth, is *manah*. Concerning the meaning of the terms "external" and "internal" some remarks will be made later on, when discussing the theory of cognition.

[45] Ab. K., i., 16, *Cittam vijanati*, Asl., p. 42 = "is aware *variously*" (M. Ting), must have the same import, if any. Cf. the Sankhya definition of *pratyaksa* in *Sankhya-karika*, 5 : *prativisay-adhyavasayo 'drstam*, where we have likewise the distributive *prati*, but *vijnana=vijnaptih*, since it is in the Sankhya system represented by the *purusa* (cf. below. Theory of Cognition), is replaced by *adhyavasaya*—the function of the internal organ (synthesis).

[46] Three *dharmas* are engaged when this kind of sensation, some times translated as "contact," is produced : *trayanam sannipatah*

with abstract objects (*mano-vijnana-dhatu*); it is the same reality, the same *dharma*. But for symmetrical arrangement it has been found necessary to have a set of three items for the purely mental elements, just as there is a three-fold set of faculty, object, and sensation corresponding to each of the Senses.[47] The difference between consciousness as a receptive faculty and the same consciousness accompanying an abstract object is then said to be a difference of time. Consciousness in the role corresponding to the place occupied in the system by the senses is the consciousness of the preceding moment.[48] The Theravadins, evidently for the same purpose of symmetrical arrangement, introduced into the system a "heart-stuff" (*hrdaya-vatthu*) which supports the non-sensuous cognitions, just as the other sense-stuffs "support" sense-cognitions. It occupies in the system the place of the sixth organ (*ayatana* or *dhatu* No. 6.)[49]

Although external in regard to one another, consciousness and mental phenomena (*citta-caitta*) were conceived as being in a closer, more intimate, connexion than other combining elements. Pure sensation (*citta*) could never appear in life in its true separate condition; it was always accompanied by some secondary mental phenomena (*caitta*).[50] Among these mental phenomena (*caitta-dharma*) or faculties (*samskara*) three are especially conspicuous, namely, feelings (*vedana*), ideas (*sanjna*), and volitions (*cetana*). In the classification into groups (*skandha*) they occupy three separate items, all the remaining ones being included together with the volitions in the *samskara-skandaha*. Feelings (*vedana*) are defined as emotions pleasant, unpleasant, or neutral.[51] Ideas (*sanjna*) are defined as operations of abstract thought, as that which "abstracts" (*udgrahana*) a common characteristic sign

sparshah (*tinnam samgati phasso*) : the consciousness (*citta*), the sense-organ, and the sense-object. Cf. below under Theory of Cognition.

[47] *Ab. K.*, i, 16, Tibetan text, p. 29, 1. 17.

[48] The mental phenomena (*caitta-dharma*) also have their objects; they are according to the current terminology *salambana*, but they are themselves *visaya* and not *indriya* (*Ab. K.*, i. 34, cf. Tibetan text, p. 49, 1.19).

[49] Cf. Mrs. C. Rhys Davids, *B. Psych.*, pp. 32, 70. This heart-stuff had, presumably, as little to do with the actual heart as the *caksur-indriya*-stuff with the actual eye. Indian Medical Science assumed the existence of a subtle *akasha*-food-stuff as a vehicle of mental processes. It is here called heart-stuff.

[50] *Ab. K.*, ii, 23.

[51] *Ab. K.*. i, 14.

(*mimitta*) from the individual objects.[52] Even the definite representation (*parichitti*) of a colour is brought under this head.[53] It is exactly what in latter Indian philosophy, Buddhist as well as Brahmanical, was understood by "definite" (*sa-vikalpaka*) cognition. Dignaga and Dharmakirti introduced into Indian logic the distinction between pure sense knowledge, free from any operation of abstract thought (*kalpanapodha*), and definite cognition (*savikalpaka*).[53] It was then adopted by Uddyotakara and the whole of the Nyaya-Vaiseshika school.[54] It now appears that Dignaga was not the originator of this doctrine, he only adapted it to his system. From the very beginning Buddhism had established this difference: *vijnana* and its synonyms *citta, manah* represent pure sensation, the same as the *kalpanapodha pratyaksa* of Dignaga, and Sanjna corresponds to definite ideas. Every construction (*kalpana*), every abstraction (*udgrahana*),[55] every definite (*parichinna*) representation, such as blue and yellow, long and short, male and female, friend and enemy, happy and miserable—this is all brought under the head of ideas (*sanjna*) as distinguished from *vijnana*=pure sensation.

Volition (*cetana*) is defined as the mental effort that precedes action. It is an element or a force which enters in the composition of a personal life (*santana*). It must not be forgotten that since there is no personality in the Buddhist outlook of the universe, there certainly is no will in our sense. *i.e.*, no personal will. There is a certain arrangement of elements, there is an element, or a force, or, still more precisely, the simply fact (*dharma*) that the elements are arranged in a certain way, according to certain laws. This fact is pointed to by the term *cetana*. It "arranges" (*sancetayati*)[56] the elements in "streams", which simple folk deem to be personalities. It is synonymous with the law of moral causation

[52] *Ab. K.* i, 14.

[53] Cf. the definition of *Pratyaksa* in *Nyaya-bindu* 1.

[54] Cf. *Nyaya-varttika, pratyaksa sutra.*

[55] *Udgrahana* is literally "abstraction," *kalpana* :"imagination," "construction". It corresponds to the part taken in Kant's system by "productive imagination," whereas *vijnana*, or the *pratyaksa* of Dignaga, corresponds to "reine Sinnlichkeit." Cf. my *Logic of Later Buddhists* (chapter on *kalpana*).

[56] To be derived from the root *ci* from which the Buddhists derive *citta* as well (Asb., p. 63) ; *sancetayati* is exactly, in form and meaning, the Russian *sochetayeti*; the Pali *adhisandahati* has the same import, cf. S. Z. Aung. *Compendium*, p. 235.

(karma)[57] and likewise with the force of vitality, the "elan vital" (bhavana, vasana), which in the Buddhist system replaces any conscious agent, whether soul or God or even a conscious human being.[58] A moment of this kind of will accompanies every conscious moment (citta).

There are, on the whole, ten mental elements which accompany every conscious moment; they are called the "general" mental elements.[59] There are ten others which are particularly "favourable for progress towards the final appeasement of life; they are faith, courage, equanimity, etc. Ten others have the contrary unfavourable or oppressive (klista) character. There are some others which have no definite moral character. All these mental elements are not general; they accompany only some of the moments of consciousness, not all of them.[60]

VII. FORCES

The definitions of the will (cetana) and of the force (samskara) are indeed the same, "what produces the manifestations (abhisamskaroti) of combining elements (samskrtam)"[61]: it is a "concerted agency."[62] Since all forces are agencies acting in some combination with other elements, we may in rendering this conception, for the sake of expediency, safely drop the word "combining" and use "forces" alone.[63] There are some indications that originally there was only one samskara in the Buddhist system, the will, and that gradually a whole catalogue of them was developed, some of the elements being entered into this group rather forcibly, with excuses.[64] The most typi-

[57] The definition of karma is cetana cetayitva ca karanam, Ab. K., iv. 1 ff., the same as in Anguttara, iii, 415; cf. Mrs. C. Rhys Davids, B. Psych., p. 93.

[58] Ab. K., ix, Soul Theory, p. 942.

[59] Citta-mahabhumika.

[60] A full list of them will be found in O. Rosenberg's Problems, p. 374, and at the end of this book.

[61] This definition we find already in the oldest sources, e.g., Samvutta, iii, 87, and it is repeated in numberless passages of the Ab. K.; cf. S. Z. Aung, Compendium, p. 236.

[62] Sambhuya-karitram, Ab., K., 1, 7.

[63] This the Buddhists themselves have also done in replacing samskrta by krtaka, cf. Nayayab, tika, pp. 47, 50 etc. A unity, without combining, can produce nothing : nu kimcid ekam ekasmat (Dignaga).

[64] In the Ab. K., i, 15, there is an interesting effort to prove that all samskaras (sixty) are included in the samskara-skandha and not cetana alone, as it would be possible to conclude from scriptural passages. As the second member of the chain of causation, samskara is equivalent to karma. Mrs. C. Rhys Davids calls my attention to the following very illuminating words in Samyutta, iii, 60 : Katama ca bhikkhave sankhara?

cal forces are the four forces of origination and decay, etc., which accompany every other element in life. Some details concerning them will be given in the sequel. In general, all elements may be divided into substances and forces (*dravya* and *samskara*). The forces are then divided into mental faculties, with the will as chief among them, and non-mental (*citta-viprayukta*) forces, among which the origination and decay forces are the most typical. But even these latter forces are sometimes given a certain amount of substantiality (*dravyatopi santi*).[65] The word and conception *samskara* performs a conspicuous part in all Indian philosophical systems. It usually means some latent mysterious power, which later on reveals itself in some patent fact. It sometimes is identified with the "unknown" (*adrsta*) conceived as a force *sui generis*. Since every philosophy is but a search for the hidden reality as opposed to the patent surface of life, the importance of the conception of a *samskara* is quite natural. Every system had its own definition and scope attributed to the connotation of this term. The Ajivika sect, as we have seen, was known by its denial of the existence of such forces. The Buddhists, on the contrary, converted all their elements into subtle forces of some degree. The subtler the element the more was it given the character of a force; but even the coarsest elements, the *mahabhutas* look more like forces than substances. There is a constant fluctuation in Buddhist terminology between a force (*samskara*) and a substance influenced by these forces (*samskrta*). A force, it must be recalled, should not be regarded as a real influence of something extending beyond its own existence in order to penetrate into another—this would be *upakara*—but simply as a condition, a fact, upon which another fact arises or becomes prominent (*utkarsa*) by itself—this is *samskara* in the Buddhist system.[66]

The little we know of the history of Indian Philosophy induces us to look to the Sankhya system as the foundation of scientific thinking. In that school the fundamental ideas were formed which sometimes unconsciously affected all later constructions. What do we find there? Three fundamental

---

Cha-y-ime cetanakaya rupa-sadda-gandha-rasa-phatthabba-sancetana dhamma sancetana ime vuccanti sankhara. According to Yashomitra, I. c., the mental faculties are included in the *samskara-skandha* because they obey the will, the other forces because they are similar to the will (*cetana*).

[65] *Ab. K.*, ii, 2, 24.

[66] Cf. the *paribhasas* to *Panini*, ii, 3, 53; vi, 1, 139; and iv, 2, 16; iv, 4, 3, in the *Kashika* (not occurring in the *M. Bhasya*), Cf. below.

principles, Matter, Mind-stuff and Energy-stuff, as interdependent moments in every real and substantial existence.
Even energy is substantial in this sense. The infinitesimals of
energy, present everywhere, are semi-material; although different from the inertia of Matter, and the luminosity of Mind,
they are separate and substantial.[67] The Buddhist elements
as infinitesimal realities, divided into elements of Matter,
Mind, and Forces, look like a reply to the Sankhya constructions from an architect of greater skill: "you maintain the
realities are *gunas*, we say they are *dharmas*." The fundamental idea of infinitesimal realities may be recognized in the
dharmas, the idea of forces everywhere present can be traced
to its origin in the Sankhya conception of *rajas;* there are
forces which are different from matter and mind (*rupa-citta-
viprayukta*). A pluralistic view of the whole is added to make
the originality of the new system, in contrast to the unitarian
tendency of the old one. But, be the case as it may, every
element of matter and mind may be called in Buddhism a
samskara, which, in this case, will stand for *samskrta-dharma.*[68]
The Buddhist idea of a force seems to be that it is the subtle
form of a substance, but even substance is here subtle enough.
The order in which the elements appear in the first classification into groups is interpreted as a gradual progress from
coarseness to subtlety: matter (*rupa*) is coarser than feeling
(*vedana*), feeling more palpable than ideas (*sanjna*), the remaining energies (*samskara*) still more subtle.[69]

The pure forces (*viprayukta-samskara*) are the most subtle
among the elements. In the loftiest, highest worlds, where
existence is entirely spiritualized, their agency continues; they
are the last to be suppressed before final extinction is reached.
The chief among them are the four forces of origination and

---

[67] Cf. B. Seal, *The Positive Sciences of the Hindus,* and S. Dasgupta, *The Study of Patanjali.* . The interpretation of the *gunas* given
there is entirely based on Vyasa who, as will be seen below, was
strongly influenced by *abhidharma.* Concerning their *mithological*
origin cf. Senart, *J. As.* 1915, v. ii, pp. 151 ff.

[68] Yaçomitra (*Ab. K.,* i., 15) remarks that the name *samskrta* is
given in anticipation, since an element will become *samskrta* only when
the forces (*samskara*) shall have exhibited their efficiency. In the
popular formula *anityah sarve samskarah* the word *samskara* stands for
samskrta-dharma. *Samskara* etymologized as *Karana-sadhana* would
mean force, and as *karma-sadhana* would be equal to *samskrta-dharma.*
The individual life, which consists of all these physical and mental elements and forces, is called *samskara-samuhah,* cf. Yaçom. (*Ab. K.,* ix),
sa, *capi Caitra-abhidhanah samskara-samuha-samtanah.*

[69] *Ab. K.,* i, 22.

destruction, etc., which are the very essence of every existence.
Then there are two forces, *prapti* and *aprapti*, which are supposed to control the collection of elements composing a personal life or to prevent (*aprapti*) the appearance in it of an
element that is not in agreement with its general character-
The Sautrantikas and Vasubandhu deny the reality of these
forces; for them they are mere names (*prajnapti*).[70] There
are two forces supposed to be active in producing the highest
degrees of trance—the unconscious trance (*asanjni-samapatti*)
and the cessation (*nirodha-*) trance or catalepsy. They are
also brought under the head of pure forces.[71] They evidently
could not be brought under the head of mind, because consciousness at that time is supposed to be suppressed. Then there
are three forces corresponding to the *sphota* of other systems.
All Indian systems contain speculations about the nature of
sound, its physical as well as its significative aspect. The physical sound was in Buddhism considered, in agreement with
the whole system, as a production, *i.e.,* (flashing) of sound-
atoms reposing on the atoms of fundamental matter. If simultaneously some atoms of translucent sound matter (*sabda-
rupa-prasada*) appeared in the ear, an auditory sensation
(*srotra-vijnana*) was produced. But the significance of the
sounds of speech was given by special forces. The Mimamsaka
school was known for its theory of transcendental, intelligible
sounds which were eternal and ubiquitous, like Platonic ideas,
and manifested themselves in the case of physical words being
pronounced. Following their fundamental principle of analys-
ing everything into minutest elements, the Buddhists imagined three separate forces which imparted to the sounds of speech
their significativeness; the force of sound (*vyanjana*), which
would seem to correspond to the modern idea of a "phonema",
the force of words (*nama*), and the force of sentences (*pada*).[72]
Generally, general ideas are also conceived as a kind of

---

[70] *Ab. K.,* ii, 37.
[71] Ibid., ii, 46.
[72] *Ab. K.,* ii, 47 ff. *Vyanjana* here corresponds to *varna, nama* to
sanjna, and *pada* to *vakya,* a case exhibiting clearly the desire to have
a terminology of one's own, so common to Indian systems : "you
maintain in the *sphota,* we say it is *vyanjana-nama-pada-samskara.*" The
real existence of these forces is admitted by the Sarvastivadin alone.
For this reason they bring the Holy Scripture under the head of
samskara-skandha, whereas the Sautrantikas classify it under *rupa,* as
sabda, and the Vijnanavadins under *vijnana-skandha;* cf. Vinitadeva's
introduction to the *Santanantarasiddhi,* edited by me in the *Bibl.
Buddhica.*

force, and it is christened by the name of *nikaya-sabhagata,* a conception intended to replace by a "force" the substantial reality of the *samanya* of other systems.[73] In general this group of forces is a rather incongruous assemblage of elements which could not be placed elsewhere. As a separate group of elements it is absent in the Theravada school. Some of its members seem to have found a place, for some reason, among the physical (*rupa*) group of that school.[74]

VIII.   NON-SUBSTANTIALITY OF THE ELEMENTS

After this succinct review of the elements of existence and their different classifications, we may consider the question as to what were they in their essence, what was the Buddhist conception of an element. The elements had four salient features: (1) they were not-substance—this refers to all the seventy-five elements, whether eternal or impermanent; (2) they had no duration—this refers only to the seventy-two impermanent elements of phenomenal existence; (3) they were unrest—this refers only to one part of the latter class, that which roughly corresponds to the ordinary man as opposed to the purified condition of the elements of a saint (*arya*); and (4) their unrest had its end in final deliverance. Speaking technically: (1) all *dharmas* are *anatman,* (2) all *samskrta-dharmas* are *anitya,* (3) all *sasrava-dharmas* are *duhkha,* and (4) their *nirvana* alone is *santa.* An element is non-substantial, it is evanescent, it is in a beginningless state of commotion, and its final suppression is the only Calm. These are what the Tibetans call the four "seals" of Buddha.[75] We now proceed to examine them separately.

ANATMA

The term *anatman* is usually translated as "non-soul," but in reality *atman* is here synonymous with a personality, an ego, a self, an individual, a living being, a conscious agent, etc.[76]

---

[73] *Ab. K.,* ii, 41.
[74] Cf. S. Z. Aung, *Compendium,* p. 157.
[75] The Southerns reckoned three "marks," evidently including the fourth in *duhkha,* as its cessation; cf. S. Z. Aung, *Compendium,* p. 210.
[76] The whole issue with every detail is admirably expounded by Vasubandhu in a concluding, ninth, chapter of *Ab. K.,* translated in my *Soul Theory of the Bouddhists.* The terms *atma, jivan, sattva, pudgala* are here used as synonyms : cf. *Soul Theory,* p. 838, and *Kathavatthu-atthakatha,* p. 8. The Vatsiputriyas made some difference between *pudgala* and *atman* ; they were *pudgalavadins,* but not *atma-vadins.* Although admitting a limited, very shady, reality of *pudgala*

The underlying idea is that, whatsoever be designated by all these names, it is not a real and ultimate fact, it is a mere name for a multitude of interconnected facts, which Buddhist philosophy is attempting to analyse by reducing them to real elements (*dharma*). Thus, "soullessness" (*nairatmaya*) is but the negative expression, indeed a synonym, for the existence of ultimate realities (*dharmata*).[77] Buddhism never denied the existence of a personality, or a soul, in the empirical sense, it only maintained that it was no ultimate reality (not a *dharma*). The Buddhist term for an individual, a term which is intended to suggest the difference between the Buddhist view and other theories, is *santana, i.e.,* a "stream," viz. of interconnected facts. It includes the mental elements and the physical ones as well, the elements of one's own body and the external objects as far as they constitute the experience of a given personality. The representatives of eighteen classes (*dhatu*) of elements combine together to produce this inter-connected stream. There is a special force, called *prapti,* which holds these elements combined. It operates only within the limits of a single stream and not beyond. This stream of elements kept together, and not limited to present life, but having its roots in past existences and its continuation in future ones—is the Buddhist counterpart of the Soul or the Self of other systems.

Consequent upon the denial of substance is the denial of every difference between the categories of substance and quality. There is no "inherence" of qualities in substance; in this respect all real elements are equally independent. As separate entities they then become substances *sui generis.* "Whatever exists is a substance," says Vasubandhu.[78] "An element is something having an essence of its own,"[79] is the current definition. To every unit of quality there is a corresponding subtle element (*dharma*) which either directly manifests itself or, according to the Sarvastivadins, remaining for ever a transcendental reality, produces a reaction (*karitva, laksana*) which we wrongly interpret as being a quality. All sense-data (*rupa*) are substances in that sense that there is no

they denied it the ultimate reality of a *dharma*; cf. *Soul Theory* and below.
[77] *Pravacanadharmata punar atra nairatmyam buddhanucasani va,* Yasom. ad *Ab. K.,* ix, in fine.
[78] *Ab. K.,* ix, *vidyamanam dravyam* : Yasom. adds *svalaksanato vidyamanam dravyam.* Cf. *Soul Theory,* p. 943.
[79] *Svalaksana-dharanad dharmah,* Yacom. ad *Ab. K.,* i, 3.

stuff they belong to. If we şay "earth *has* odour, etc.", it is only an inadequate expression; we ought to say "earth is odour, etc.", since besides these sense-data there is absolutely nothing the name could be applied to.[80] The same principle is applied to the mental sphere; there is no spiritual substance apart from mental elements, or faculties, that are conceived as subtle realities or substances *sui generis*, very much on the same pattern as the elements of matter.[81] There is no soul apart from feelings, ideas, volitions, etc.[82] Therefore an element technically means "non-self."[83]

IX. PRATITTYA-SAMUTPADA (CAUSALITY)

Although the separate elements (*dharmas*) are not connected with one another, either by a pervading stuff in space or by

[80] *Prthivi gandhavatity ukte rupa-gandha-rasa-sparseghyo nanya darsayitum sakyate*, Yasom, ad *Ab. K.*, ix; cf. *Soul Theory*, p. 742.

[81] In his *History of Indian Philosophy* (Cambridge, 1922), p. 244 Professor S. Dasgupta maintains that in Sankhya philosophy there is likewise no separate existence of qualities (i.e., no inherence of qualities in a substance). This is based (as the learned author informs me in a letter) on *Vyasa*, iii, 12 (*sapeksiko dharma-dharmi-bhavah*) and Vachaspati's comment. There are other passages suggestive of a similar idea, e.g., *dharmi-svarupa-matro hi dharmah* (ibid., iii, 13). But it is added *dharmi-vikriyaiva esa dharma-dvara prapancyate*. In Buddhism there cannot be any change of *dharmin*, since everything is new at every moment. Besides it must not be forgotten that Vyasa, as will be shown later, was strongly influenced by the Abhidharmists. If Professor S. Dasgupta's views that the ultimate entities in Sankhya were called *gunas*, probably to suggest that they are the entities which by their various modifications manifest themselves as *gunas* or qualities, is accepted, this would constitute a very strong analogy between the Sankhya *gunas* and the Buddhist *dharmas*. In his *Vijnanamatra-siddhi* Vasubandhu applies the term *dharma* to the *tattvas* of the Sankhyas (O Rosenberg).

[82] It is a matter of surprise how long it has taken European science to realize this doctrine, which is so clearly stated in numberless passages of Buddhist writ, and in one of them even in terms very nearly approaching to Hume's statement (*Samyutta*, iii, 46): "all Brahmans or Sramanas who attentively consider the soul, which so variously has been described to them, find either the five groups of phenomena (physical, feelings, ideas, volitions, or pure sensation) or one of them," etc. The stumbling-block has always been the supposed theory of transmigration of souls and its "glaring" contradiction with the denial of soul. Buddhism always had two languages, one for the learned (*nitartha*) and one for the simple (*neyartha*).

[83] *Ab. K.*, ix, cf. *Soul Theory*, p. 840, where it is stated that *anatma* is synonymous with 5 *skandhas*, 12 *ayatanas*, and 18 *dhatus*, i.e., with all *dharmas* : a single *dharma* is likewise synonymous with *nihsattva*. It is, therefore, misleading to translate Buddhaghosa's interpretation of *dharma=nissatta, nijjiva*, as meaning "inanimate thing," as Mrs. and Prof. Geiger have done, op. cit.. (Unbelebtes, Ding. Sache). Since consciousness itself and all mental phenomena and even Nirvana are *dharmas*, Buddhaghosa could not have meant that they are "inanimate things" in the ordinary sense of the word. The compound *nissatta* must be explained either as a *madhyama-pada-lopi—nirgatah sattrah*, or as a *bahuvrihi—nirgatah sattvo yasmat*.

duration in time, there is, nevertheless, a connexion between them; their manifestations in time, as well as in space, are subject to definite laws, the laws of causation. These laws bear the general name *pratitya-samutpada*. We have seen that connotation of the word *dharma* implies the meaning of elements operating together with others. This concerted life of the elements (*samskrtatva*) is but another name for the laws of causation—the combined origination (*sam-utpada*) of some elements with regard (*pratitya*) to other elements.[84] Thus it is that the fundamental idea of Buddhism—*the conception of a plurality of separate elements*—includes the idea of the *most strict causality* controlling their operation in the world-process. The "theory of elements"—the *dharmasanketa*, says Vasubandhu, means that "if something appears, such and such result will follow"—*asmin sati idam bhavati*.[85]

The most popular form of the laws of causation is represented by the theory of the twelve consecutive stages in the ever revolving stream of life from birth to death; it is, so to say, the vertical line of causastion, while other relations represent the horizontal.[86]

[84] Yacom, ad *Ab. K.*, ii, 45 : *samskrtatvam pratitya-samutpannatvam iti paryayavetau*; *sametya sambhuya pratyayaih krtam samskrtam*; *tam tam pratyayam pratitya samutpannam, pratitya-samutpannam iti.*

[85] *Ab. K.*, iii, 18 and 28, cf. also ii, 47, and ii, 50.

[86] The interpretation of this formula has been the crux of European scholars, while in Buddhist countries, as O. Rosenberg certifies, it is supposed to be very plain and accessible to the simplest understanding. The right explanation, in the light of the *dharma* theory, will be found in O. Rosenberg's *Problems*, chap. xvi. The stumbling-block to every explanation came from the supposition that the formula was meant to represent some evolution in which one member was producing the other; it was then impossible to deduce e.g., *nama-rupa* from *vijnana*, unless the latter be taken in the sense of the *buddhi* of the Sankhyas. In reality, as soon as the first moment of life (*vijnana*—third *nidana*) appears, all the eighteen *dhatus* are already present, according to the principle "there is no *citta* without *caitta*, and no *bhuta* without *bhautika*." On *vijnana* as the first moment in the life of the embryo. cf. *Ab. K.*, i, 35, Tibetan, p. 62, 6, and i. 22, Tibetan, p. 47, 18, and also Mrs. C. Rhys Davids, *B. Psych.*, p. 25. The number of *tattvas* in an embryo, according to Sankhya, is likewise eighteen, though there is difference in counting. According to Charaka (*sharirasthana*, iv) the sperm-cell of the father contains minute particles of all the organs. Consequently *vijnana*, as the third member in the "wheel of life", is a *technical term* indicating the first moment of a new life arising out of pre-natal forces (*avidya, samskara*). The next seven members mark the stages of the development of the embryo into a child, youth, and grown-up man. The trsna-stage corresponds to sexual maturity, when new *karma* begins to be formed. The two last members refer briefly to future life. The ideas that all elements are present through the whole process, the difference being only in the relative "prominence" (*utkarsas tvabhivyanjakah*, cf. Susruta, *Sutrasthana*, xii) of one element over the others, points out to Sankhya habits of thought, where everything was

In the popular literature of the Sutras the term *pratitya-samutpada* is almost exclusively applied to this formula of the "wheel of life," although the general meaning of it must have been present to the mind of all Buddhists. It is implied in the division of *dharmas* into *ayatanas,* which is founded on the theory that knowledge arises (*samutpadyate*) when conditioned (*pratitya*) by an object and a receptive faculty. "All *abhidharma* is but an interpretation of the sutras" the current definition says. Therefore the general meaning of the idea of "interconnected origination of elements" may have appeared in the *abhidharma* by a sort of generalization founded on actual conceptions that are to be found in the sutras in a somewhat different form. This question is directly asked by Vasubandhu. "Why is it," says he, "that the twelve members of interconnected origination of the elements are differently treated in the Scripture and in the Exegesis? e.g. it is stated in the latter that the interconnected origination of elements (*pratitya-samutpada*) is a term equivalent to all the active elements (*samskrta-dharma*)?" And he answers : "Because in the sutras this relation is treated intentionally (in a popular way, with reference to the development of an individual's life), whereas the exegetical works explain its essence (in regard to all elements in general).[87]

Some of the causal relationships have already been mentioned. Thus the relation of simultaneity (*sahabhu*) ties together the four fundamental and the secondary elements of matter—*bhuta* and *bhautika.* The same relation applies to the simultaneous origination of consciousness and mental phenomena (*citta and caitta*). But for the vice versa conjunction—one would be tempted to say "inherence" if it was not so grave a mistake against the fundamental principle of Buddhism—of the mental elements with pure consciousness (*citta*), a specific, more intimate, association was imagined. Evidently there was a feeling that the various mental facts were more closely united with consciousness than the atoms of matter with one another. This fact received the name of *samprayoga,* i.e., a thorough and intensive union, and it was explained as *anuparivartana,* i.e., a following and enveloping

considered immutable, always existing (*sarvam nityam*), all things entering in one another (*sarvam sarvatmakam*), the difference being only a passing manifestation of some element, while the others continued to assist in a latent state.

[87] *Ab. K.*, iii, 25, Cf. O. Rosenberg, *Problems*, p. 223.

of consciousness by concomitant mental phenomena or the secondary mental elements (caitta). It must not be imagined that this close connexion of consciousness with other mental elements means any unity between them, allowing only a logical distinction for purposes of analysis, as in modern psychologies. A Buddhist element is always a separate entity, it is neither "compound" nor "phenomenon," but an element (dharma). The close connexion, "envelopment" or consciousness by other mental elements only means that they are its satellites, they appear and disappear together, they are produced by the same causes, and have the same moral aspect.[88] Ten such satellites are the minimum number to accompany consciousness (citta) at every moment; a feeling, an idea, a volition, some attention, some understanding (mati = prajna), some concentration (samadhi) etc., are always present in every conscious moment.[89] They are conjoined, but conjoined by the law of "satellites" (samprayoga).[90]

The Sarvastivadin school reckons in all six different causal relations, but in these details the schools varied a great deal, and they evidently represent a later development of the original idea. The detailed account given in the Abhidharma-kosha represents the doctrine in its final form which it received in the abhidharma of the Sarvastivadins.

X. KARMA

One of the most illuminating features of Buddhist philosophy is its deep research into the phenomenon of moral causation. All Indian systems contain an appeal to the "unknown" (adrsta, apurva) as a transcendental cause which has to be posited in explaining the origin and the ultimate goal of life. The Buddhists distinguish between (1) causation among ele-

---

[88] Ab. K., ii, 52, reckons ten different ties of the "satellites" with citta. The Theravada seems to reckon only four, cf. Asl., p. 42 : ekuppadadinam vasena sampayogattho vutto.

[89] The number is then increased by the four samskrta-laksanas of each element, and by the four laksanas and four anulaksanas of citta itself, thus making fifty-eight satellites the minimum number to unite in every single ksana with citta, the fifty-ninth (Ab. K., ii, 52).

[90] The figurative words of Buddhaghosa (quoted by Mrs. Rhys Davids, B. Psych., p. 54) are apparently intended to describe this kind of union. That vijnana is the most general mental element is admitted by all Buddhists; but that it "includes and involves other elements, let alone aggregates, has never been admitted in abhidharma—it would be pure vijnana vada. The samprayoga connexion is known to Buddhaghosa; cf. Asl. p. 42. The Ab. K., i, 35, Tibetan, p. 62, 9, argues that, if the mental phenomena were not different from citta, they would not have been called caitta.

ments of dead matter, where the law of homogeneity (sabhaga-helu) between cause and result reigns, (2) causation in the organic world, where we have the phenomenon of growth (upacaya), and (3) causation in the animate world, where the operation of moral causation (vipaka-hetu) is superimposed upon the natural. The elements constituting the stream of our present life are conditioned, in addition to the natural course of events, by the mysterious efficiency of past elements or deeds, if the latter have possessed a moral character of some force or prominence. The different activities of everyday life have no such efficiency. But a prominent deed, whether good or bad, will affect the whole stream and may carry its result either at an early or very remote date. The resulting event (vipaka-phala) is always indifferent (avyakrta) in the moral sense, because it is a natural outflow of a previous cause, and is supposed not to be produced voluntarily. This moral law is also called karma.

The influence of karma is not in the Buddhist outlook so overwhelming, controlling the whole universe; as it is in other non-Buddhist systems, and as it also becomes, under the name of vasana, in the later idealistic systems of Buddhism also. In abhidharma it is one of the forces controlling the world process: it is the chief force so far as it controls its gradual progress towards Final Deliverence. Its operation is subject to the following conditions. Every fact produced by the "matur-ing influence" (vipaka) of moral or intellectual antecedents (karma) necessarily belongs to animate life (sattvakhyah) but is by itself morally indifferent (avyakrto dharmah). It is in-different because it is a natural outcome of antecedents, it always arrives involuntarily, automatically. If something is produced voluntarily, it may become the starting point of a new development. When it has an outspoken strong moral character, whether good or bad, it becomes karma, and will have corresponding consequences which, again, will appear automatically, since they are fully foreshadowed by their ante cedents and are not voluntary acts. This explains the defini-tion of Karma, as given by Vasubandhu: Karma is will (cetana) and voluntary action (cetayitva karanam).[91] Exactly the same difinition is found in the Pali canon, and evidently was current in Buddhism from the beginning.[92]

[91] Ab. K., iv, 1 ff.
[92] Anguttara, vol. iv., 415.

When a new life is produced, its component elements, i.e., the eighteen classes (*dhatus*) of elements, are present, although in an undeveloped condition. The first moment of the new life is conventionally called *vijnana*. It constitutes the third member (*nidana*) of the ever revolving "wheel of life." Its antecedents are *karma*, i.e., the good or bad instincts" sticking to it from the beginning. In the formula of the "wheel of life" this member appears under the name of *samskara*, i.e., pre-natal forces. Another, more general, antecedent is *avidya*, the first member of the wheel, representing the defiling influence (*klesa*) of ignorance and other vices, the absence of discriminating knowledge (*prajna*). Among the components (*dhatu*) of the new life ten represent matter. They are atomic. The atoms are compound atoms, they contain the usual eight components with addition of particles of sensibility-stuff (*rupa-prasada*) or "orannic"-stuff (=*indriya*). The "tangibility"-stuff (*kayendriya*) pervades the whole body. In some parts of the body, e.g., in the organ of vision, the atoms have a still more complicated structure. But not only does matter consist of compound atoms, it consists of momentary appearances of atoms. In dead, inorganic matter one moment follows the other, obeying solely the law of uniformity or homogeneous production (*sabhagaja*). The next moment follows automatically (*nisyanda*) on the former one. There is neither growth nor decay. This uniform course would represent the Buddhist counterpart of what we might call eternity of matter, Although the same matter is also present in the organic body, nevertheless the term "uniform course" (*sabhaga-hetu*) cannot be applied to it in that condition. It is reserved for those cases where there are no other causes in addition to the uniform sequence of moments constituting inorganic matter. When other processes—the process of growth (*upacaya*), the influence of intellectual and moral causes (*vipaka*)—are superimposed upon the uniform course of the existence of matter, when it belomes organic and living, the consecution of its moments receives other names (*upacayaja*, *vipakaja*). The pure "uniformity-relation" between consecutive moments—the *subhaga-nisyanda*-relation —obtains only in the realm of inorganic, dead matter. When the atoms of organic matter have assembled, the phenomenon of growth (*upacaya*) becomes the controlling principle of development, the atoms increase in number. This process of growth is supported by favourable circumstances: good food (*anna-visesa*), quiet sleep (*svapna-visesa*), physical tidiness (*samskara-visesa*), and careful behaviour (*samadhi-visesa*). But this growth is not the only factor which controls the development of living bodies. The influence of what we may term heredity steps in, and is superimposed upon the natural process of growth. This is the influence of *karma*, the maturing (*vipaka*) influence of moral antecedents. When the organs of the body are being formed, or are developing, this influence conditions their final constitution. The question is then raised, what is the mutual relation of these two different agencies, natural development and heredity? The answer is that the first process constitutes the "vanguard," or a rampart, under the protection of which the second, the *vipaka*, may safely operate.[93] It is not quite easy to realize what such an answer may exactly mean. At any rate, it suggests a more subtle, spiritual, or semi-spiritual character of the second force. *Karma* is not quite physical (*paudgalika*) with the Buddhists, as it is with the Jains, but it seems to be semi-physical, since it interfers in the disposition of atoms along with the principle of growth that accumulates them.

A very interesting illustration of the meaning of these Buddhist conceptions about heredity, retribution, etc.,—all facts falling under the head of *karma-vipaka*—is given by the following scholastic question. Voice is always produced voluntarily, consequently it cannot be the product of moral antecedents, of *karma*. It is not *vipakaja*, for all the facts of heredity are produced automatically (*nisyanda*). But we know that the Great Man (*mahapurusa*) i.e. a Buddha, has a captivating, melodious voice, a noble elocution. It is one of the characteristic gifts of a Buddha, and is due, like all his sublime qualities, to heredity, i.e. to a long course of moral progress running through generations. Therefore his extraordinary voice and elocution must likewise be a consequence of his moral antecedents (*vipakaja*). The puzzle is solved by assuming a double causality. The configuaration of atoms in his organs of speech was influenced by heredity, i.e. moral causes (*vipakaja*), but his actual speech is a voluntary, not an automatical act, and therefore could not be interpreted as a

[93] *Ab. K.*, i, 37, ' and Yacom.—*upacaya-santana vipaka-santanasya parivara-avasthanenaiva araksa.*

direct product of his sublime nature, or the result of his former achievements.[94]

The elements of moral defilement (klesa) are always present in a life (santana), in a latent or patent condition. When latent they have the form of "residues" (anusaya), they stick to the other elements, pollute them, bring them into commotion and prevent their coming down to rest. This influence of the disquieting elements in life is termed "general cause" (sarvatraga-hetu) because it affects the whole of the stream of life (santana), all its elements become soiled. The primary cause of this unhappy condition is "illusion" (avidya), the first, fundamental member in the wheel of life. It continues to exist and exhibit its influence as long as the "wheel" turns, and is gradually neutralized and finally stopped by an antidote in the form of transcending wisdom (prajna amala). Some details about this process will be given later on when dealing with the "unrest" of the elements. This process of gradual extinction of the klesas and the consequent purification of life is the ultimate aim of the Buddhist doctrine. For the sake of it the analysis of life into elements, the research into their functions, and connexions was undertaken: sanklesa-vyavadanikam idam sastram—this ' doctrine is a doctrine about defilement and purification, or, more exactly, about the commotion and final apeasement of life.[95]

Although emphatically banned from the dwelling of Buddhist philosophy and replaced by the laws of inter-connexion, the conceptions of substance and quality seem to have found a back-door through which partly to re-enter in their usual position. For the division of the elements of matter into primary and secondary (bhuta bhaulika) and of the mental elements into fundamental and derivative (citta and caitta) approaches very nearly the relation of substance and quality. The secondary are supported (asrita)[96] by the primary, and this connexion is inseparable; the one cannot appear without the other. In the Buddhist interpretation they are, nevertheless, separate elements although linked together by the laws of causation. A special relation of simultaneous or reciprocal

[94] Ab. K., i, 37, Tib text, pp. 65 ff.
[95] The second part of the second Kosa-sthana contains an exposition of the hetu-pratyaya theory. Cf. also Ab. K., i, 35—6, Tibetan text, pp. 64 ff.
[96] The derived elements of matter are called upadaya-rupa, i.e. bhutani upadaya; cf. the discussion under Ab. K., i, 35.

causation (*sahabhu*) is then imagined to save the situation. In theory the one element is as much the cause of the other as the latter is the cause of the former.* The mental phenomena are not included in consciousness (*citta*), but are standing by it, mutually they are enveloping (*anuparivartante*) it, but, nevertheless, they are separate elements.* Notwithstanding these efforts to maintain their equal rights, we see that the attempt has not been successful, since there is a primary and secondary position; the secondary is spoken of as supported by the primary and their connexion is inseparable. It is presumably for this reason that Buddhadeva, one of the celebrities of the Sautrantika school, revolted against such inequality of treatment, and denied the difference between primary and secondary elements; he maintained that all were equally primary (*bhuta* and not *bhautika*).* But this stricture had no success; it was disposed of by reference to the Scriptures and by pointing, as it would seem, to the prominence of the tactile sense-data; the general manifestations (*laksana*) of matter—repulsion, attraction, heat, and motion—are all tactile phenomena, and they are general,[99] whereas colour etc., can be apprehended by vision alone. Moreover, the translucent matter of .the sense organs could not exist (i.e., appear) without being backed by some more consistent forces.[100]

XI. IMPERMANENCE OF THE ELEMENTS

The elements of existence are momentary appearances, momen-

---

[97] *Ab. K.*, ii, 51

[98] It is curious that the *citta* is related to *caitta* by he *sahabhu* relation, which is defined as mutual causality, one member being the cause of the other as much as the latter is the cause of the former. Nevertheless, the *caittas* stand to *citta* in another relation,* called *samprayoga*. They "envelop" the *citta*, but do not enter into it, for this would mean "inherence," which is prohibited. Through the cobweb of these devices one can clearly watch the apparition of the ghost of the Soul, which it has cost so much effort to ban.

* *Ab. K.*, i, 35.

[99] Charka (*sharirasthana*, chap. i) likewise points out that the *laksanas* of his five *bhutas* are tactile phenomena—*sparc-endriya-gocaram*.

[100] Buddhadeva in his turn quotes the *Garbharakranti-sutra* (not to be traced in the Pali canon) and a passage stating that at the conception moment of Buddha (i.e., the third *nidana*, technically called *vijnana*) the embryo was *saddhatuka*, i.e. consisting of six elements, *vijnana*, four *mahabhutas*, and *akasha*; the *bhautikas* are not mentioned. But it is answered that the *mahabhutas* are alone mentioned, since *bhuta* represents the *bhautikas* as well, and *vijnana* is here equivalent to *citta* and *caitta* (*Ab. K.*, i, 35, Tibetan text, p. 62,• 6 ff). Sushruta (*Sutra-sthana*, xii) has the same view as Buddhadeva. He likewise shares the view that the prominence, *utkarsa*, not the quantity, of one kind of atoms, determines the class of the compound.

tary flashings into the phenomenal world ont of an unknown source. Just as they are disconnected, so to say, in breadth, not being linked together by any pervading substance, just so are they disconnected in depth or in duration, since they last only one single moment (*ksana*). They disappear as soon as they appear, in order to be followed the next moment by another momentary existence. Thus a moment becomes a synonym of an element (*dharma*), two moments are two different elements. An element becomes something like a point in time-space. The Sarvastivadin school makes an attempt mathematically to determine the duration of a moment.[101] It, nevertheless, admittedly represents the smallest particle of time imaginable. Such computations of the size of the atom and of the duration of a moment are evidently mere attempts to seize the infinitesimal. The idea that two moments make two different elements remains. Consequently, the elements do not change, but disappear, the world becomes a cinema. Disappearance is the very essence of existence; what does not disappear does not exist.[102] A cause for the Buddhists was not a real cause but a preceding moment, which likewise arose out of nothing in order to disappear into nothing.

It is at present impossible to determine the epoch when this theory was definitely framed. Some of the oldest schools, at any rate, expressed it very clearly.[103] They maintained that mountains, trees, the elements of matter, all elements in general, were momentary apparitions, like moments of thought. The schools differed on this point, and the complete logical demonstration was constructed, probably, at the time when logic had taken the place of *abhidharma*.[104] But it is easy to

---

[101] *Ab. K.*, iii, 15, cf. S. Z. Aung, *Compendium*, p. 25.

[102] Thus existence becomes synonymous with non-existence, since every fact disappears at the same moment when it appears; this is the Indian way of expressing the idea developed by H. Bergson ; *Creative Evolution*, p. 2.: "the truth is that we change without ceasing, and that the state itself is nothing but change." The conclusion of Bergson is to the indivisibility of duration, whereas the Buddhists stick to the separate moments and make them appear out of nothing—*asata utpadah*—and again disappear into nothing—*niranvaya-vinashah* ; cf. *Nyayabindut*, p. 68. *Vedanta-sutra*, ii, 2, 6, and *Samkhya-sutra*, i, 44-5, accuse the Buddhists of converting existence into non-existence.

[103] *Katharatthu*, xxii, 8 ; *eku-citta-khanika sabhe dhamma*.

[104] The ancient term seems to have been *anitya*, which is accepted by all schools. It was replaced in the sequel by *ksanika*. This may reflect some change in the definiteness of the view. The logical argument is that every moment being a different determination, must be a separate entity : *riruddha-dharma samsargad dhy anyad vastu*, cf. *Nyayabindu'*

realize that, given the fundamental Buddhist idea of the plurality and separateness (*prthakatva*) of their elements this idea, worked out with the characteristic Indian intrepidity in philosophical construction, must have been carried to its logical consequence, i.e., the assuming of no duration, since there was no stuff that could possess duration.

A consequence of this doctrine was a denial of motion. A really existing object, i.e., an element, cannot move, because it disappears as soon as it appears, there is no time for it to move. This does not contradict the circumstance that one of the general characeristics of matter, the fourth *mahabhuta*, is motion. Every motion is resolved in a series of separate apparitions, or flashings, arising in contiguity to one another.[105] Motion of physical objects, as explained in the *abhidharma*, gave the best support to the consideraion of dead matter as a series of evanescent flashings. The phenomenon of acceleration of falling bodies is explained by a difference in the intensity of the element, weight or motion (*irana*) at every moment of its downward course since the object at every moment is differently composed.[106] An element is thus comparable to a fire, it consists of a series of separate flashings following one another, every moment representing a new fire.

The Sarvastivadins construe the theory of the momentary character of the elements in the following manner.[107] Every element appearing in phenomenal life is affected simultaneously by four different forces (*samskaras*), the force of origination (*utapada*), decay (*jara*), maintenance (*sthiti*), destruction (*anityata*).[108] These forces affect every element at every moment of its existence, they are the most universal forces, the characteristic features or the manifesting forces of pheno-

---

tika, p. 5 (*Bibl Ind.*). By the conversion of the proposition *yat sat tat ksanikom* it was proved that, if something did not disappear, it did not exist. The doctrine is fully expounded in Ratnakirti's *Ksanabhangasiddhi* (Six Buddhist Tracts, *Bibl. Ind.*), and is controverted in numerous Brahmanical works.

[105] *Ab. K.*, iv, 2, *na gatir, nashath*, it is not *kriya*, but *nirantara-utpada*, see below, under Theory of Cognition, p. 45.

[106] *Ab. K.*, ii, 46. The Vaishesika admit one indivisible *samskara* till the cessation of a motion. This would correspond to Bergson's idea of the indivisibility of motion. The Naiyayikas, on the contrary, admit as many *samskaras* as there are momentary *kriyas*.

[107] It is expounded with all details of the issue between Sautrantikas and Sarvastivadins by Vasubandhu in *Ab. K.*, ii. 46. Prof. L. de la Vallee Poussin has kindly communicated to me his French translation of this important text, which I compared with my own English translation,

[108] Sometimes reduced to three—birth, subsistence and decay.

menal existence (samskrta-laksanani). The elements affected
by them are called the manifested elements (samskrta-dharma).
Unaffected by them are only the three elements of eternal
unchanging existence (asamskrta-dharma). The term samskrta
is therefore synonymous with ksanika, i.e., impermanent or
momentary.[109]

According to the laws of interconnexion between elements,
these four forces always appear together and simultaneously.
They are sahabhu.[110] Being elements themselves, they are in
need of secondary forces (upalakshana) in order to display
their efficiency. The realistic tendency of the Sarvastivadins, if
there was any, consisted in constructing some realities corresponding to our ideas or habits of speech. This tendency they
shared with the Nyaya-Vaisesika system. Just as the latter
had a quality of conjunction (samyoga) as something real,
additional to the things which were joining, just so the
Sarvastivadins had their origination, decay, existence, and
destruction in addition to the elements originating and disappearing at the same moment. They insisted that these four
forces, and the secondary potencies influencing them in their
turn, were realities (dravyatah santi). Against this idea of an
element which was simultaneously originating, existing, and
disappearing, the very natural objection was raised by all the
other Buddhist and non-Buddhist schools that production and
destruction could not be simultaneous. On the other hand, it
was impossible to allow an element more than one single
moment's duration, since two moments constituted two
elements. The Sarvastivadins met the objection by pointing
to the difference between an element in itself, its real nature
(svabhava) and its efficiency-moment, its function, or manifestation (karitva laksana). The elements or forces may be opposed
to one another, yet their effect may result in some single real
fact, as e.g., supposing three assassins have resolved together
to kill a man hiding in some dark recess, one of them, (utpada)
pulls him out of his hiding place (the future), the other seizes
him, the third stabs him, all acting simultaneously. The
victim (dharma) appears only to disappear. The reality

[109] The translation of samskrta-dharma as "compound" is a contradic-
tio in adjecto. A dharma is never compound, it is always simple. Where-
ever there is composition there are several dharmas.

[110] Just as the chitta never appears without simultaneously being accompanied by chaitta-dharmas, or the four mahabhutas appearing simultaneously with the bhautikas.

moment is the moment of action, of its being achieved. "We call a moment," the Sarvastivadins maintain, "the point when an action is fully achieved."[111] We have here the germ of the later idea that this moment is something transcendental, something that cannot be expressed in a discursive thought.[112] The moment was then raised to the position of the "thing in itself,"[113] the transcendental foundation of reality; indeed, the absolute reality itself[114]—a conception which had great importance in the development of later Indian philosophy.[115]

The Sautrantika school takes a more simple and reasonable view of the question. They deny the reality of the four manifestation-forces of production, decay, etc.[116] The corresponding notions of production, destruction, etc., refer, not to single moments, but to series of them (santana).[117] Even if applied to one moment these notions do not imply the existence of corresponding realities, they are mere names for the fact that a momentary entity appears and disappears.[118] This entity itself appears and disappears, there is no need of supplementary forces for this. Consequent on that, a further very important divergence between the two schools arises. As stated above, the Sarvastivadins maintain that all elements exist on two different planes, the real essence of the element (dharma-svabhava) and its momentary manifestation (dharma-lakshmana). The first exists always, in past, present, and future. It is not eternal (nitya) because eternality means absence of change, but it represents the potential appearances of the element into phenomenal existence, and its past appearances as well. This potentiality is existing for ever (sarvada asti). Even in the suppressed state of Nirvana, when all life is extinct, these elements are supposed to represent some entity, although its manifestation-power has been suppressed for ever. The future potential elements are, indeed, divided in this

---

[111] *Kriya-parisamapti-lakshmana eso nah ksanah, Ab. K.*, ii, 46; cf. Nyayabindutika, p. 13. (*Bibl. Ind.*) : *ksanike vastuni...eka-kriya-karitvena sahakari grhyate.*

[112] *Ksanasya (jnanena) prapayitum asakyatvat* (ibid. p. 16).

[113] *Svalaksana,*, ibid.

[114] *Paramartha-sat,* ibid.

[115] Dharmakirti identified the moment with pure sensation, where subject and object coalesce, and the Vedantins deemed that we have in this moment a direct perception of *Brahma.* The Indian astronomers and mathematicians knew the differential conception of instantaneous motion of a planet, *tatkaliki gatih,* a motion constant during an infinitesimally small interval ; cf. B. Seal, *Positive Sciences of the Hindus,* p. 77.

[116] *Dravyato na santi,* cf. *Ab. K.*, ii, 46.

[117] Ibid.   [118] Ibid.

school into two different sets, those that will appear (*utpatti-dharma*) and those that are suppressed and never will appear (*anutpatti-dharma*). Since the moment (*kshana*) is not something different from the element (*dharma*), time in general is not different from the elements taken collectively, as far as they have not lost their capacity of appearing in phenomenal life. In fact, "the times" is one of the synonyms used to designate collectively the elements appearing in ordinary life.[119] But the term "time" (*kala*), implying the reality of one time, is carefully avoided; it is replaced by the term "transition" (*adhvan*). When the Sarvastivadin maintains that "everything exists", it means that all elements exist, and the emphasis which is put on the reality of elements refers to the conception that their past as well as their future transition represents something real. From this fundamental tenet the school derives its name. Since the conception of an element answers rather to our conception of a subtle force than of a substance, the reality, i.e. effectiveness of the past is not so absurd as it otherwise would appear. The Sautrantikas denied the reality of the past and the future in the direct sense, they admitted the reality only of the present. The future, they contended, was not real before becoming present, and the past was not real after having been present.[120] They did not deny the influence of past facts upon present and remote future ones, but they explained it by a gradual change in an un-interrupted sequence of moments, this sequence having a starting-point in a conspicuous or strong impinging fact; it was for them one of the laws of interconnexion between separate elements.[121]

There was another school which occupied an intermediate position between the Sautrantikas and Sarvastivadins; it maintained the reality of the present facts and of that part of the past ones which had not already lost their influence, but the reality of the future ones and of that part of the past ones which had ceased to exhibit any influence it denied. Vasubandhu calls this school the Vibhajyavadins, or Distinguishing School.[122] The whole argument between the rival

---

[119] *upadana-skandha*, cf. *Ab. K.*, i, 7, Tibetan text, p. 12, 6.
[120] *Ab. K.*, v. 24 ff., cf. Appendix. 1.
[121] *Ab. K.*, ix, cf. *Soul Theory*, p. 949.
[122] In the *Kathavatthu*, i, 8, such opinions are ascribed to the Kacyapiyas. These also admitted the reality of that part of the future which was foreshadowed or fixed by the past or present. Hiuen Thsang states

schools is presented by Vasubandhu with every detail in
his usual masterly manner and need not be repeated here.[123]

XII. IMPERMANENCE IN SANKHYA-YOGA

The depreciation of "change and decay" and its contrast with
something that "changes not" is a popular theme, with many
religions and philosophies. The merit of having worked it
out up to the remotest logical consequences appertains to
Buddhism. It appears that in this work the Buddhists were
assisted by the parallel work of Brahmanical philosophers of
the Sankhya-Yoga school. The starting-point of the latter was
just the reverse of the Buddhistic one. They maintained a
unity of existence, cause and effect were one in essence. But
a corollary of the unity of substance (satkarya-vada) was the
constant change of its manifestations; this change was also
conceived as momentary (pratiksana-parinama). The moment
is here defined as the infinitesimally small measure of time,
just as the atom is the smallest imaginable fraction of matter.[124]
Two moments cannot coalesce,[125] therefore there is no real
duration, no time outside the moment.[126] Time is an idea
without reality, an empty construction of the mind.[127] The
only reality is the momentary thing. The past and the future
are not real directly, but, since the present cannot exist
without a past, the latter is inherent in the fact of change.[128]
"Therefore," says Vyasa, "the whole universe is included in
one single moment, all the real units of change you may
imagine[129] are merged in every single moment."[130] Concluding, Vyasa admits two kinds of eternity, immutable eternity
belonging to the soul and eternity of mutation belonging to
matter.[131] The unit of change is termed dharma, and it is
identified with the moment (kshana) in Yoga as well as in
Buddhism. The change of manifestation was called a change
of dharma;[132] but in the Brahmanical system it is quite natural

---

in his Commentary that the Kacyapiyas are here meant under the name
of Vibhajyavadins (McGovern). The Theravadins seem to have shared
the same opinions as the Sautrantikas. The explanation of vibhajya-vada
as orthodox or analytic school because Buddha himself was vibhajya-
vadin (cf. Kathavatthu, introduction) seem to be unknown to Vasubandhu.
[123] Cf. translation in Appendix I.
[124] Vyasa's Bhasya, ad iii, 52.   [125] Ibid.
[126] Ksana-tatkramayor nasti vastu-samaharah, ibid.
[127] Vastusunyo buddhinirmanah, ibid.
[128] Parinamanvitah, ibid.   [129] Ibid, ami sarve dharmah.
[130] Ibid, tatksanoparuddhah.
[131] Ibid, iv., 33.   [132] Ibid, iii, 13.

to make use of this term, since an old and usual meaning of
it is "quality", and in the Sankhya view the changing manifestations are appurtenances of some pervading stuff. It is
therefore probable that the technical meaning of this term
in Buddhism developed from one of its old meanings, with
the difference that, quality being left without any support by
the substance, it became an independent quality, or quality
in the role of substance. As in the Buddhist system, these
manifestations are conceived as forces (sakti)[133] and even
potential forces (yogyatavacchinna)[134] corresponding to the
Buddhist conception of a samskara. The difference is that
they belong to some substance (dharmin). The reality of
"transition-time" (adhvan) as distinguished from a "duration-
time" (kala) was admitted; the same term—adhvan—is used on
both sides to express the first of these conceptions.[135]

If we turn to the Sarvastivadin view, which admitted some
transcendental everlasting reality of the elements along with
their passing manifestations, the similarity becomes still more
striking, and the difference is often restricted to the wording.
A dharma, says Vyasa, exists in all the three times.[136] The
manifestation (dharma) and the manifested (dharmin) are quite
the same, the manifestation represents only the way in which
the manifested appears.[137] The reality of the past and the
future is then proved by Patanjali and Vyasa in almost the
same expressions that are used by the Sarvastivadins,[138] with
the difference that there is no mention of separate forces
(samskria-laksanani) of production and destruction. When
accused of drifting into Sankhya, the Sarvastivadins justified
themselves by pointing to these momentary forces which saved
the Buddhist principle of detached entities.[139]

The question of the relation between the permanent
essence of an element and its manifestation was thoroughly

---

[133] Vyasa's *Bhasya*, iii, 14.   [134] Ibid   [135] Ibid., iv. 12.
[136] Ibid., iii, 13.   [137] Ibid.
[138] The Sarvastivadins argue that the past and the future must exist
because we have knowledge of the past and of the future objects : this
knowledge cannot be of non-existence, i.e., of nothing. We find quite the
same argument in *Vyasa-bhasya* ad iv. 12. cf. Appendix I. Stress is laid
upon the conception *adhvan* "transition", when the reality of past and
present are asserted : *adhva-vishistataya sattvam trayanam apy arishistam*
(Vachaspati ad *Vyasa-bhasya*, iv. 12). This reality is inherent in the fact
of transition : *ye tu bhuta-bhavinah ksanas te parinamanvita vyakhyeyah*
(Ibid., iii. 52). Otherwise there would be contradiction between iv. 12
and iii. 52, where it is said : *na purvottara-ksanah santi*.
[139] Cf. Appendix I.

discussed among Buddhists, and four solutions were suggested. The first belonged to Dharmatrata:[140] it maintained unity of substance (dravya) along with a change in existence (bhava). This was dismissed by simply pointing to the obvious fact that this was Sankhya and not Buddhism. The second explanation belonged to Ghosa; it assumed that elements, although existent in the past, present and future, changed their aspect (lakshmana) or intensity, accordingly as they appeared at different times; just as the passionate love for one woman is only an intensification of a feeling which is alive towards women in general; it does not mean total absence of this feeling in other cases. This explanation was not accepted on the ground that it implied co-existence of the different aspects at the same time. Vasumitra advocated a change of condition (avastha), i.e., of efficiency (karitva) in the present, and non-efficiency in past and future. This view was accepted in the school as the correct one. It was illustrated by the ball of an Indian abacus: being thrown in the hole for units it means one, in the hole for hundreds-hundred, etc. Finally Buddhadeva thought that past, present, and future were contingent (apeksa) upon one another, just as the same woman may be a mother with respect to her child and a daughter with respect to her mother. This was dismissed as leading to a confusion of the times. The passage of the *Vibhasa*, where these opinions of four celebrated masters of the Sarvastivadin and Sautrantika schools were reported, enjoyed apparently great popularity. Reference is made to it in later Buddhist works,[141] and it evidently was borrowed from the Buddhists by Patanjali and Vyasa. *Yogasutra*,[142] aims at giving an explanation of the time variations of one substance; it adopts the suggested explanations not as exclusive of one another, but as subordinate and co-existent. The change of manifestation (dharma) is characterized further on as a change of aspect (lakshmana) and condition (avastha). The characteristic examples for illustrating the suggested explanations are repeated in Vyasa's *Bhasya* with slight modifications. As though answering the variety of the Buddhist theories, Vyasa emphatically maintains that the change of quality (dharma), aspect (lakshmana) and condition (avastha) is but the same

---

[140] Cf. Appendix I.

[141] As e.g. in Bhavya's account of the sects : cf. Rockhill's *Life of Buddha*. [142] iii, 13.

fact variously described. "There is, therefore," says, he, "only one kind of mutation of matter, though variously described by us............The mutations of external aspect of time-variations (*lakshmana*) and of intensity (*avastha*), as here described, do not transcend the substance as such. Hence there is only one kind of mutation which includes all those varieties we have described."[143] Buddhadeva's theory that the time variations are contingent upon one another, which logically leads to the conclusion that essence and manifestation are interchangeable terms, may have influenced the somewhat similar theory of Patanjali and Vyasa that substance and quality are contingent (*sapekshika*) terms.[144]

The doctrine of momentary universal change originated probably in the Sankhya system. From this doctrine it receives the name of a Theory of Change—*parinama-vada*, which is only a natural corollary of its fundamental principle of unity between cause and effect (*satkarya-vada*). It is natural to surmise that early Buddhism has been influenced by it. But in a later period the Sarvastivadin philosophers unquestionably exercised a considerable influence on the formation of the Sankhya-Yoga doctrine.[145]

XIII. UNREST OF THE ELEMENTS

The third salient feature of Buddhist elements is that they represent *duhkha*, a term which has always been rendered by suffering, sorrow, etc. Sufficient as this interpretation may be for popular literature, it is evident that theoretically something else is meant. Such expressions as "the element of vision (*chaksuh*) is sorrow,[146] "all elements influenced (*sasrava*, i.e., influenced by desire to live) are sorrow"[147]—an element "colour" might be brought under the head of "sorrow" as well[148]—could not be understood if our usual idea of sorrow

---

[143] Cf. Professor J. H. Woods' translation in his *Yoga System of Patanjali* (Harvard O. S.) p. 217.   [144] *Vyasa*, iii, 15.

[145] The point of similarity between the Buddhist system and the Sankhya-Yoga, especially as presented in the *Yoga-Sutra* and *Bhasya*, are so overwhelmingly numerous that they could not escape the attention of the students of *abhidharma*. Some of them have been occasionally noticed above. The point deserves special treatment. Professor de la Vallee Poussin has kindly communicated to me in MS. a paper prepared by him on the subject. He also informs me that Professor Kimura in Japan has arrived at the same conclusions independently from him.

[146] *Ab. K.*, i, 19, Tibetan text, p. 31, 5.

[147] Ibid., i., 9, Tibetan text, p. 13, 6.

[148] Because it is entered into the *upadana-skandhas*, a synonym of which is *duhkha* and *duhkha-samudaya* (Ab. K., i, 8, Tibetan text,

was brought in. The idea underlying it is that the elements described above are perpetually in a state of commotion, and the ultimate goal of the world process consists in their gradual appeasement and final extinction. The old Buddhist credo (*ye dharma hetu-prabhavah*) already expresses the idea very sharply: "the Great Recluse has indicated the (separate) elements, their interconnexion as causes and effects, and their final suppression."

Vasubandhu likewise[149] states that Buddha in his compassion for the troubles of mankind offered them a means of salvation which did not consist of magic or religious boons, but of the knowledge of a method of converting all *utpatti-dharmas* into *anutpatti-dharmas*, i.e. of stopping for ever the commotion created by the operation of the forces active in the process of life.[150] Our conception of a Buddhist element (*dharma*) would not be complete if this connotation of a commotion to be suppressed (*heya*) were not included, along with its non-substantiality and momentary evanescence.

This feature converts the *dharma*-theory into a doctrine of salvation—the chief aim of theoretical as well as practical Buddhism. The doctrine amounts shortly to the following details. From the view-point of a gradual progress towards Final Deliverance all the elements of life may assume two different characters: they either are characterized by a tendency towards life, commotion and turmoil, and then they are called *sasrava*,[151] i.e. "influenced" by passions; or they are "uninfluenced" (*anasrava*), i.e., they exhibit the opposite tendency towards reduction of life, appeasement of commotion and even

---

B. W.). The translation of *arya-satya* by "Aryan facts" (M. Ting and Mrs. Rhys Davids) is evidently better than the old translation "truth". What is really meant is a distribution of the elements (*dharma*) into four stages, unrest (*duhkha*) and its cause (*samudaya*), final appeasement (*nirodha*) and its cause (*marga*), a formula of elements corresponding to every stage. The *sasrava-dharmas* are the same as *duhkha* and *samudaya*, the *anasrava-dharmas* the same as *nirodha* and *marga*; cf. *Ab. K.*, i, 3. Thus *duhkha* in this formula does not at all mean "sorrow", but it is a synonym of the seventy-two *dharmas*, or the five *upadana-skandhas*. Its general meaning is exactly the same as the meaning of the formula *ye dharma*. This *duhkha* is *parinama-duhkha*. Evidently Ledi Sadaw had this conception in view when pointing to the difference between two kinds of *duhkha*; cf. Mrs Rhys Davids, *B. Psych*, p. 83. Cf. S. Schayer, *Mahayanistische Erlosungslehren*, p. 6.

[149] Ad *Ab. K.*, i, i.   [150] *Ab. K.*, i, 1.
[151] Cf. *Ab. K.*, i, 3. The derivation of the word from the root *sru* is, no doubt, correct, as is proved by the Jaina view of the *karma* matter "flowing" into the body through the pores of the skin.

annihilation.[152] The passions (klesha), being themselves
separate elements, i.e., represented as substantial entities, affect
the stream of life (santana) to which they belong. Roughly, the
first set of elements (the sasrava-dharmas) correspond to the
ordinary man, with all his enjoyments and bothers in life; the
second make up the saint (arya), who stands aloof from all
interest in life and cares only for Final Deliverance. A
thorough knowledge, a discrimination,[153] of all elements of
existence is essential for Salvation, since when they are known
they can be singled out and gradually suppressed one after
the other. The connotation of the term "element" (dharma)
thus includes three further conceptions: (1) it is something
that can be well determined, i.e., distinguished in the complex
stream of life as an ultimate reality; (2) this something is in
a state of eternal commotion; (3) it is something that must
and can be appeased, and brought to an eternal standstill.[154]

A special element received in this connexion extraordinary
prominence. It is termed prajna, which may roughly be
translated "understanding." It is one of the chitta-mahabhu-
mika elements, i.e., a mental faculty always present, in every
conscious moment. In the ordinary plane of existence it is
synonymous with mati and means simple understanding, the
capacity of appreciating something. But it is capable of
development and becomes then prajna amala, "immaculate
wisdom," anasrava prajna, "understanding uninfluenced (by
mundane considerations)." Its presence gives the whole
stream (santana) a special character, it becomes the central
element of the stream, and its satellites—all other elements of
the "stream"—feelings, ideas, volitions, become pure.[155] The
presence of this element acts as an antidote against other
elements that are "unfavourable" (akusala) for progress; they
gradually disappear and cannot reappear in the same stream.
The first thing to be realized in such a state is the theory of
the elements (dharmata), the idea that there is no permanent

[152] The eternal asamskrta elements are included among the anasrava
class (Ab. K., i, 3).
[153] Ab. K., i, 2., dharma-pravicaya—a through picking out of elements
one by one.
[154] In the terminology of abhidharma "something to be suppressed"
means that it is an element (dharma); cf. Ab. K., i, 15, Tibetan text,
27, 8. If something is not mentioned among the objects to be suppressed,
that means that it is not a dharma; cf. Ab. K., ix, Soul Theory, p. 844.
Something to be "well known, thoroughly known" means lsikewise that
it is a dharma (ibid., p. 837).
[155] Ab. K., i. 2, and Yasom. comment.

personality (*pudgala, atma*), that the supposed personality
really is a congeries of eighteen components (*dhatu*). When
the wrong view of an existing personality (*satkaya-drsti*) is disposed of, the path that leads to Final Deliverance is entered.
Every vicious, or disquieting, "unfavourable" (*akusala*)
element has a special antidote in the agency of wisdom; when
suppressed it becomes an *anupatti-dharma,* an element which
never will return, a blank is substituted for it; this blank
(*nirodha*) is called "cessation through wisdom" (*pratisankhya-
nirodha*).[156] But only the initial stages of saintliness can be
reached through this so-called *drsti-marga,* i.e., through knowledge a certain amount of *dharmas* has its flashings stopped.
The remainder are stopped by mystical concentration, they are
bhavana-heya,[157] i.e., to be suppressed by entering the realms
of trance. In all Indian systems the ultimate instrument of
salvation is Yoga. This can not only do away with the intellectual and moral elements that are "unfavourable", but can stop
the existence or appearance of matter itself. We have seen
that matter is reduced in this system to sense-data, which are
conceived rather as forces, momentary flashings. Practical
observation has shown to the philosophers that when a certain
degree of intense concentration is reached the sensations of
taste and smell disappear, hence, it is concluded, the objects,
the sense-data of odour and taste, have likewise vanished.
Founded on this practical observation, a plane of existence has
been imagined,[158] where living beings of "streams" (*santana*)
consists only of fourteen instead of eighteen components.[159]
In the *Abhidharma-kosha* the question is raised, how many
elements can be suppressed through knowledge and how many
through ecstasy? and it is answered that some mental elements

---

[156] *Pratisankhya* is synonymous with *prajna amala;* it is the same as
the *prajna* or *prasankhyana* in the Sankhya-Yoga system, an agency
destroying the *klesas.* It was probably the original meaning of the
word *samkhya,* from which the system received its name. The Buddhist
specification in the way of the preposition *prati* refers to the separateness
of the elements, of which every one needs a separate action of wisdom
in order to be suppressed: cf. *Ab. K.,* i, 4. The same tendency is
probably responsible for the term *prati-moksa* instead of *moksa,* as
prati-vijnaptih, cf. above. p. 14: the term *prati-buddha,* on the contrary,
is used as a designation of the "Enlightened One", in the Upanisads
(cf. H. Oldenberg, *Die Lehere dur Upanishaden,* p. 131) by Jains,
Sankhyas, but not by Buddhists.

[157] *Ab. K.,* i, 20.

[158] *Ab. K., bhasya,* ad i, 30, Tibetan text, p. 53, 4, where this explanation is attributed to Srilabha, and is, evidently, shared by Vasubandhu
himself.

[159] The *dhatus* Nos. 8-7 and 14-15 are in abeyance.

are suppressed by mere knowledge only, namely, the belief in a real personality (sat-kaya-drsti) and its consequences—all the feelings, ideas, and volitions and forces connected—they disappear as soon as the antidote, i.e. the anatma=dharma-theory, is realized. Other impure elements (sasrava), all the material elements (dhatus 1—5 and 7—10), and all sensuous consciousness (dhatus 13—17; fifteen dhatus in all) can be suppressed only by ecstasy.[160] Since matter was conceived as a play of subtle forces, its disappearance in a manner similar to the suppression of passion and wrong view is not so illogical. The purified elements of the saint (anasrava-dharma) could not be suppressed at all, but they likewise disappeared at the time of Nirvana, through absence of new karma, i.e., elements of unrest (duhkha), to which the commotion of the world was due. Imagination has constructed whole worlds where these kinds of matter and sensations corresponding to them are absent, they are the worlds of reduced, or purified, matter.[161] They can be entered either by rebirth in them (utpatti), or by an effort of concentration (samapatti), an absorption which transports into higher planes of existence not merely Buddhists. Working further on upon the same principle, higher worlds are constructed where the material side—the sense-data experience further reduction and finally worlds purely spiritual are reached, where every matter, i.e. all sensations and sensa-data are absent. Speaking technically, the formula of a living being in these planes of existence will reveal only three component terms (dhatu) : consciousness (mano-dhatu), mental phenomena and forces (dharma-dhatu), and abstract, non-sensuous cognition (mono-vijnana-dhatu).[162] These purely spiritual beings (or, more precisely, formulas of being) have their consciousness and mental phenomena brought to a standstill at some very high planes of transic existence: the unconscious trance (asanjni-samapatti) and cessation trance (nirodha-samapatti). But this is, nevertheless, not an eternal extinction. At last the absolute stoppage of all the pure dharmas of the highest spiritual beings is reached, an eternal blank is substituted for them. This is Nirvana, absolute annihilation of the samskrta=dharmas, which is tantamount to the presence of the asamskrta-dharmas.

According to the Sarvastivadins, this quite negative result is, nevertheless, an entity of some kind. They make a difference, as stated above, between the essence and the manifesta-

---

[160] Ab. K., i, 40.   [161] Ab. K., i. 30, rupa-Dhatu.   [162] Ab. K., i, 31.

tions of the *dharmas*. At the time of Nirvana the manifestations have ceased for ever, there will be no rebirth, but this
essence remains. It is, nevertheless, a kind of entity where
there is no consciousness.

Thus the ultimate goal of the world-process, the final result
of all purifying, spiritualizing agencies and efforts is a complete
extinction of consciousness and all mental processes. The
absolute (*nirvana*) is inanimate, even if it is something. It is
sometimes, especially in popular lierature, characterized as
bliss, but this bliss consists in the cessation of unrest (*duhkha*).
Bliss is a feeling, and in the absolute there neither is a feeling,
nor conception, nor volition, nor even consciousness. The
theory is that consciousness cannot appear alone without its
satellites, the phenomena of feeling, volition, etc.[163] and the
last moment in the life of a *bodhisattva*, before merging into
the absolute, is also the last moment of consciousness in his
continuity of many lives.[164] The appeasement of wrongs and
passions is the general ideal of humanity; but this appeasement
carried further on and raised to the state of absolute insensi-
bility is a peculiarity of the Hindu ideal. Philosophy has
converted that into conceptual formulas, and the result may
seem absurd, but "whosoever wishes to be a philosopher must
learn not to be frightened by absurdities," says a distinguished
modern author.[165] Buddhism was not the only Indian system
of philosophy to arrive at such a result: in the Vaishesika
system the liberated soul is as inanimate as a stone (*pasanavat*),
or as ether (*akasavat*), because cognition, feeling, etc., are not
considered as of its essence, but as an accidental quality produced by special contacts, which cease when final deliverance
is reached.[166] The absolute is spiritual only in those systems
which accept the doctrine that consciousness is of the essence
of the absolute, i.e. the doctrine of self-luminosity (*sva-prakasa*)
of knowledge.[167]

XIV. THEORY OF COGNITION

The character of a philosophical system generally comes forth
very clearly in its theory of cognition; it enables us to assign

---

[163] *Ab. K.*, ii. [164] Ibid., i, 17, Tibetan text, p. 30, 5.
[165] Bertrand Russell, *Problems of Philosophy*, p. 31.
[166] Cf. references in A. B. Keith's *Indian Logic*, p. 261 n. •
[167] Clearly expressed by Dharmakirti in the celebrated verse :
avibhago hi buddyatma...

it a place among either the realistic systems, maintaining the reality of the outer world, or among the idealistic ones, denying such reality. Among the Indian systems we find every variety of such theories represented. The Nyaya-Vaishesika system favoured a naively realistic view of a series of real contacts of the object with the sense-organ, of the latter with an internal organ, which in its turn entered into contact with the soul, and thus cognition was produced. The Buddhist idealistic school of Dignaga and Dharmakirti developed a transcendental theory which exhibited some striking points of similarity with the transcendental theory of Kant. The Sankhya-Yoga system would explain the origin of knowledge through an assumed assimilation of the mind-stuff to the object, through the medium of a sense-organ, compared with the attraction of an object by a magnet.[168] Even later Vedanta, notwithstanding its strictly monistic principle, managed to establish some kind of realistic view about "seizing" the object by the senses.[169] What was, as compared with these views, the conception of earlier Buddhism, that part of Buddhist philosophy which admitted the existence of elements (dharma) as ultimate realities, i.e. the Sarvastivadins and the Sautrantikas ?

Their explanation of the origin of knowledge was in perfect agreement with their ontology, i.e. with the theory of a plurality of separate, though interdependent, elements (dharma). The phenomenon of knowledge was a compound phenomenon, resolvable into a number of elements simultaneously flashing into existence. Being conceived as momentary flashes, the elements could not move towards one another, could not come into contact, could not influence one another, there could be no "seizing" or "grasping" of the object by the intellect. But, according to the laws of interconnexion (pratitya-samutpada) prevailing between them, some elements are invariably appearing accompanied by others arising in close contiguity with them. A moment of colour (rupa), a moment of the sense-of-vision-matter (chaksuh), and a moment of pure consciousness (chitta), arising simultaneously in close contiguity, constitute what is called a sensation (sparsa)[170] of colour. The element of consciousness according to the same laws never appears alone,

---

[168] *Yoga Sutra*, i. 4, 7.
[169] *Vedanta-sara*, 29.
[170] *Trayanam sannipatah sparsah.* It is misleading to translate *sparsa* by "contact", since it represents a *chaitta-dharma*.

but always supported by an object (*vis̠aya*) and a receptive faculty (*indriya*).[171]

A very important, though somewhat scholastic, question is then raised; how is it that, if these three separate elements—the element colour, the element visual sense, and the element consciousness merely appear, or flash together, without being appurtenances of some non-existing living being, without being able to influence one another, to "grasp", apprehend, or come into contact with one another—how is it, then, that there, nevertheless, is an "apprehending" of the object by the intellect? Why is it that the resulting knowledge is a cognition "of colour", and not a cognition of the visual sense, which is supposed to enter the combination on terms of equality with the other elements? The question about the relation between external (objective) and internal (subjective) element, and the "grasping" of the one by the other which was to have been evaded by the construction of a plurality of interdependent, but separate and equal, elements, reverts in another form. The answer is that, although there is no real coming in contact between elements, no grasping of the objective element by the intellect, nevertheless the three elements do not appear on terms of absolute equality; there is between two of them—consciousness and object—a special relation which might be termed "co-ordination" (*sarupya*),[172] a relation which makes it possible that the complex phenomenon—the resulting cognition—is a cognition of colour and not of the visual sense.

Such an answer amounts, of course, to a confession of ignorance; this relation exists because it exists, it is required

[171] *Chaksuh pratitya rupam cha chaksur-vijnanam utpadyate.* Here *chaksur-vijnana* is not a visual sensation—that would be *sparsa*—but a pure sensation, arising accompanied by a moment of the visual-sense-matter.

[172] This same *sarupya* reappears in the transcendental system of Dignaga and Dharmakirti, as it would seem, in a different, but similar, role of a salvage in extremis. Dharmakirti establishes an absolute reality, the thing in itself, the single moment of pure sensation (*suddham pratyaksam = kalpanapodham = svalaksanam = ksana = paramarthasât*); this single moment of reality is the transcendental (*jnanena prapayitum na sakyate*) reality underlying every representation with its complex of qualities, constructed by imagination (*kalpana*). There is a difficulty in supplying some explanation of how this quite indefinite moment of pure sensation combines with the definite construction of reason, and *sarupya* steps in to save the situation. Its role is consequently similar to Kant's schematism, that was intended to supply a bridge between pure sensation (reine Sinnlichkeit) and reason. Cf. my *Logic according to later Buddhists*, chap. on *pratyksha*. About *sarunva* in Sankhya-Yoga see below.

by the system, without this patchwork the system collapses. In all Indian—and, indeed, not only Indian—systems we always reach a point which must be acquiesced in without any possible justification. It must be assumed, not because it could be proved (na sadhayitum sakyam), but because there is no possibility of escape (avarjaniyataya), it is a postulate of the system (siddhanta-prasiddham).

In the Abhidharma-kosha we have the following account of the process of cognition : [173]

Question—We read in scripture, "Consciousness apprehends." What is consciousness here meant to do?

Answer—Nothing at all. (It simply appears in co-ordination with its objective elements, like a result which is homogeneous with its cause.) When a result appears in conformity with its own cause it is doing nothing at all; but we say that it does conform with it. Consciousness, likewise, appears in co-ordination (sarupya) with its objective elements. It is (properly speaking) doing nothing. Nevertheless, we say that consciousness *does* cognize its object.

Question—What is meant by "co-ordination" (between consciousness and its objective elements)?

Answer—A conformity between them, the fact owing to which cognition, although caused (also) by the activity of the senses, is not something homogeneous with them. It is said to cognize the object and not the senses. (It bears the reflection of the objective element which is its, corollary.) And, again, the expression "consciousness apprehends" is not inadequate, inasmuch as here also a continuity of conscious moments is the cause of every cognition. ("Consciousness apprehends" means that the previous moment is the cause of the following one.) The agent here also denotes simply the cause, just as in the current expression "the bell resounds" (the bell is doing nothing, but connected with it every following moment of sound is produced by the previous one.) (We can give) another (illustration) : consciousness apprehends similarly to the way in which a light moves.

Question—And now does a light move?

Answer—The light of a lamp is a common metaphorical designation for an uninterrupted production of a series of flashing flames. When this production changes its place, we

---

[173] Ab K.., ix; cf. *Soul Theory*, pp. 937-8.

say that the light has moved, (but in reality other flames have
appeared in another place). ·Similarly, consciousness is a
conventional name for a chain of conscious moments. When
it changes its place (i.e. appears in co-ordination with another
objective element) we say that it apprehends that object. And
in the same way we are speaking about the existence of
material elements. We say matter "is produced", it exists,
but there is no difference between existence of an element
and the element itself that *does* exist. The same applies to
consciousness, (there is nothing that *does* cognize, apart from
the evanescent flashings of conciousness itself).

The question of the reality of an outer world is, strictly
speaking, obviated. In a system which denies the existence
of a personality, splits everything into a plurality of separate
elements, and admits of no real interaction between them, there
is no possibility of distinguishing between an external and
internal world. The latter does not exist, all elements are
quite equally external towards one another. Nevertheless, the
habit of distinguishing between internal and external, subjective
and objective, could not be dropped altogether, and we meet
with curious situations into which the philosopher is driven by
logical deductions; consciousness itself sometimes happens to be
considered as an external element with regard to other elements.
Such elements as ideas (*sanjna*), feelings (*vedana*), volitions
(*chetana*), and all forces (*samskara*), are, as a rule, considered
to be external elements. The *Abhidharma-kosha* gives the
following account of the question: [174]

Question—How many among the eighteen categories of
elementary components (*dhatu*) of life are internal, how many
external?

Answer—Internal are twelve, (the remaining six) colour,
etc., are external.

Question—Which are the twelve internal ones?

Answer—They are the six varieties of consciousness
(*sadvijnana-kayah*), i.e. consciousness (1) visual, (2) auditory,
(3) olfactory, (4) gustatory, (5) tactile, (6) purely mental, and
their six respective bases (*ashraya*): the sense-organs of vision,
audition, smelling, tasting, touch, and consciousness itself, i.e.
its preceding moment (being the basic elements of the next
moment)—are internal. The remaining six, comprising visi-

[174] *Ab. K.*, i, 39.

4

bility matter (sounds, smells, tastes, tangibles, and mental or abstract objects, e.g. ideas) are external.

Question—How is it possible for the elements of existence to be internal or external, if the Self (or the personality) in regard to which they should be external or internal does not exist at all?

Answer—Consciousness is metaphorically called a Self, because it yields some support to the (erroneous) idea of a Self. Buddha himself uses such expressions. He sometimes mentions control of the Self, (sometimes control of consciousness) e.g. "the wise man who has submitted *his Self* to strict control, migrates into heaven," and (in another place) He says: "the control of one's *consciousness* is a weal, the control of *consciousness* leads to bliss." The sense of vision and other sense-organs are the basic elements for the corresponding sensations; consciousness, on the other hand, is the basic element for the perception of a Self. Therefore, as a conse- quence of this close connexion with consciousness, the sense- organs are brought under the head of internal elements.

A very characteristic question is then raised, namely, that this definition of an internal element does not apply to consciousness itself. If to be internal means merely to be the basic element of consciousness, as the organ of vision e.g. is the basic element (*acraya*) for any visual consciousness, then, since consciousness could not be its own basis, it could neither be an internal element. The question is solved by stating that the preceding moment of consciousness is the basis for the following one, and since time is irrelevant in this definition, consciousness must also be called internal. In any case, the *dharmah* or *dharma-dhatu*, i.e. ideas and all mental phenomena and forces, are supposed to be external elements,[175] that is a postulate of the system.

The theory sketched above does not by any means prevent our using the expressions of common life with regard to an inter-action or contact between sense-organ and object. We meet even with the comparison of this contact to a clash of

---

[175] The exact division of the eighteen *dhatus* from this view-point is in—(1) Six bases, *acraya-satka*, *caksuradi*: organs of sense and con- sciousness (*manah*), otherwise called *sad indriyani*, or the six faculties. (2) Six "based", *acrita-satka*, *caksur-vijnanadi*: five varieties of sensa- tion and intellectual consciousness (*mano-vijnana*). (3) Six cognized objects (*alambana-satka* and *visaya-satka*): five varieties of sense objects and mental objects; they are, with regard to the second set, *alambanas*, and *visayas* with regard to the *indriyas*.

butting goats, but these expressions need not be taken literally. About the possibility of any real contact between the sense-organ and its object, we find the following explanations.[176] The senses are divided into two sets according to their power of acting at a distance, or through contact only. The senses of vision and audition apprehend their objects at a distance. For the eye a distance is even a necessary condition, because e.g. a drop of medicine introduced into the eye cannot be seen by it. The three organs of smelling, tasting, and touch must be in immediate contact with the object. The question is then raised, how is contact possible if there is no movement, and it is answered that contact is only a name for production of two elements in immediate vicinity. The question of contact between object and organ of sense affords an opportunity for debating the question of contact between objects in general. The Vaibhasikas maintain that when there is a contact, i.e. simultaneous production of two things in close vicinity, their vicinity is absolute, there is nothing between, but Vasubandhu objects that absolute vicinity is impossible for many reasons. He quotes the opinion of two celebrated philosopheres, Vasumitra and Bhadanta; the first says: "If the atoms of which the objects are composed could really come into contact, they would be existing during the next moment," i.e. since every atom is but a momentary flashing, its coming into contact is impossible; the contact will be achieved by another atom appearing in the next moment. Bhadanta says: "There is no such thing as contact. Contact is only a name for the close vicinity (of two apparitions)".[177]

With regard to matter (rupa), the Abhidharma-kosha gives two different standpoints from which to consider its position as either external or internal. It is external if part of another's personality (samtana), his faculties or his objects, internal if part of my own personality, my faculties or my objects. Otherwise it may be distinguished according to the classification into ' bases" (ayatana) of cognition. As we have seen, this classification divides everything according to the faculties by which it is perceived: the five sense-organs (indriya) are internal bases (adhyatmayatana) and the objective sense-data represent the external ones (bahyayatana).[178]

[176] Ab. K., ad i, 43, Tibetan text, p. 82, 5 ff.
[177] Nirantara-utpada, ibid, Tibetan text, p. 83, 9.
[178] Cf. Ab. K., i, 20. For the position in the Pali canon cf. Mrs. C.

Since there is no real difference of external and internal, the senses do not really play any part in perception; they are mere facts or elements that appear together with other elements according to laws of interconnexion. If we speak of the sense of vision as perceiving colour, this must not be taken literally. There is in the *Abhidharma-kosha*[179] a long discussion about the relative parts of the two elements, of the visual sense and of consciousness, in the process of perception. First an idealist opponent maintains that consciousness alone produces cognition, the part of the senses is *nil.* This opinion is disposed of by pointing to the fact that consciousness does not apprehend objects behind a wall, which it ought to have achieved if it were independent of the sense-organs.[180] The Sarvastivadin then reviews several explanations of the difference between the parts of the sense-organ and consciousness in preception. "We find in Scripture", he says, "the following statement":

"This, O Brahmin, is the organ of vision; it is a door through which to see colours and shapes." This means that consciousness perceives (colours) through the organ of vision (which is comparable to a door). It, strictly speaking, means that when we use the verb "to see" we only indicate that there is an (open) door (for the consciousness to apprehend a colour). It is wrong to maintain that the organ of vision (*chaksuh*), "looks" (*pasyati*), with the result that it "sees", (perception is produced only by the element of consciousness).

Question.—If it is the element of consciousness that "sees", who is it that becomes conscious (of the thing seen)? What is the difference between these two expressions, "to see a colour" and "to become conscious of the presence of a colour"?

Answer.—Although that (element) which produces consciousness cannot, strictly speaking, be supposed "to see", nevertheless both expressions are used indiscriminately: "he sees" and "he is conscious of", just as with regard to understanding (*prajna*) we may equally use the expressions "he sees it" and "he understands it."

The Sarvastivadin then states that the elements of visual

Rhys Davide, *Buddhist Psychology*, p. 140 ff. The idea that external matter is the matter entering into the scope of another person's life may be traced in the *Vibhanga*, where exterior *rupa* is said to be the interior *rupa* of another person : *rupam bahidha yam rupam tesam tesam parasattanam* (? *parasam-tananam*) *parapuggalanam*, etc. Cf. likewise Majjhima, i, 421 ff. (No. 2 Maharahulovadasutta).

[179] *Ab. K.*, i, 42, Tibetan text, p. 77, 10 ff.

[180] Ibid., Tibetan text, 78, 11 ff.

sense and consciousness do not exhibit any agency, they simply appear under certain conditions: the organ of sense and the object being present, consciousness arises, and the mere fact of its apparition is tantamount to a sensation of colour, just as the sun in arising produces the day; it does nothing, but its appearance itself is the day. The Sautrantika adheres to the same opinion, and winds up with the remark : "What is the use of this quarrel about 'who sees' and 'who is conscious'? It is like chewing empty space ! A visual perception (sensation) is a fact, conditioned by two other facts, an organ of vision and some colour. Which is the agent? What is the agency ? Useless questions ! There is nothing but the elementary facts (*dharma-matram*) appearing as cause and effect. In practice, according to the requirements of the case, we may use either the expression 'the eye sees' or 'consciousness is being aware'. But we should not attach great importance to these expressions. Buddha himself has declared, 'do not stick to the expressions used by common people, do not attach any importance to usual terms!' The eye sees, 'the ear hears,' 'the nose smells,' 'the tongue tastes,' 'the body feels,' 'the intellect becomes conscious,' the Kashmirian Vaibhasikas make use of these expressions (without taking them literally).[181]

This sounds like an answer to the Sankhya philosophers. They maintained that the sense organ "sees," but consciousness "is conscious."[182] The Mimamsakas adopted the same view in admitting an indistinct sense-perception (*alochana*) comparable to the perceptions of a child and the clear vision with participation by the understanding.[183] The transcendental school of Dharmakirti denied the difference. It maintained that, distinct or indistinct, the fact of knowledge remained the same in its essence.[184]

There is no great disagreement between the Vaibhasikas (Sarvastivadins) and the Sautrantikas on the interpretation of the origin of cognition. It is in their opinion a complex phenomenon in which several elements participate, interconnected, but separate, with the essential presence of the element of consciousness among them.[185]

[181] *Ab. K.*, i, 42, Tibetan text, p. 79, 18.
[182] Garbe, *Sankhya Philosophie*, 2nd ed., pp. 319 fl., 326.
[183] *Clokavartika, Pratyaksasutra*.
[184] *Nyayabindut.*, p. 4 ff.
[185] The information about the Sautrantika theory of cognition, contained in the *Sarva-darshana-sangraha* and similar works (*bahyarthanu-*

In the light of this theory of cognition it is surprising to
see the family-likeness which reveals itself between the consciousness (*chit, purusa*) of the Sankhya and its Buddhist counterpart
(*vijnana*). Both are absolutely inactive, without any content, a
knowledge without an object, a knowledge "of nothing," pure
sensation, mere awareness, a substance without either qualities
or movements. Being the pure light of knowledge it "stands
by" the phenomena, illuminates them, reflects them, without
grasping them or being affected by them.[186] The only difference is that in Sankhya it represents an eternal principle,
whereas in Buddhism momentary light-flashes appearing at the
time when certain other elements are present[187] The order
which it occupies among the Buddhist groups (*skandhas*) of
elements is likewise suggestive. It is not included in the
mental groups. It has a place of its own just at the end of the
list, similar to the position occupied by it as the twenty-fifth
principle of Sankhya.[188] In order to avoid the difficulty involved in the idea of one element "grasping" the other, it is
imagined that there is the mere fact of them being near one
another.[189] Whatsoever that may mean in Yoga, in Buddhism
it refers to interconnected flashings into existence of two elements. Their relation of subject and object, nevertheless,
remains unexplained, and this fact is christened by the name
of "co-ordination" (*sarupya*). We meet the same *deus ex
mahina* performing an analogous task in both systems; subject
and object stand aloof from one another, yet they are "co-
ordinated."[190]

It can hardly be doubted that the emphatic denial of any
difference between consciousness, mind, and intellect[191] in
Buddhism is likewise a direct reply to the Sankhya system,
where we find such a gap between consciousness and mind,
and the latter then divided into the threefold internal organ.

meyatva), reposes on a confusion by Brahmanical authors between
Sautrantika and Vijnana-vada, not seldom to be met with.

[186] Garbe, op. cit., pp. 358 ff.

[187] *Sankhya-karika*, 64, which has given an opportunity to impute to
the system the negation of a soul, only proves that the conscious principle deprived of any characteristic or content, represents in Sankhya
nothing else than pure sensation, or pure consciousness. Cf. Garbe, op.
cit., p. 364.

[188] About the order in which the *skandhas* stand we find a great many
speculations in *Ab. K.*, i, 22; cf. Mrs. C. Rhys Davids, *B. Psycho.*, p. 54.

[189] Vyasa, ad i, 4 : ii, 23.

[190] Prof. J. H. Wood translates "correlation", which is much the
same (op. cit., p. 14, 160 ff).

[191] *Ab. K.*, ii, 34; Mrs. C. Rhys Davids, *B. Psych.*, p. 66.

The doctrine of identity between consciousness and an internal organ of knowledge is characteristic for Buddhism from its very beginning. It is, in fact, another manner of expressing the denial of a soul and is the direct consequence of its being replaced by separate elements. We find it clearly stated in the oldest texts.[192] It probably was, at the time, a new doctrine, intended to replace an older one. The pre-Buddhistic use of the terms is clearly discernible in the Pali texts. One or the other of these synonymous terms is used with preference in certain contexts.[193] As an organ (indriya, ayatana No. 6) and as a common resort (pratisarana) for the sense-organs, the term "mind" (manah) is preferred; consciousness purely mental, non-sensuous, is called manovijñana (dhatu No. 18), i.e. consciousness arising, not from an organ of sense, but from consciousness itself, from its preceding moment, when the preceding moment takes the place of a support (asraya) or an organ (indriya), for a non-sensuous idea. These distinctions are mere traces of older habits of thought. The philosophical atmosphere in the time of Buddha was in all probability saturated with Sankh'ya ideas. Buddhism cannot be fully understood if these connexions are not taken into account.

XV. PRE-BUDDHAIC BUDDHISM

Can the theory sketched above be characterized as a system of realism? It is certainly not the naive realism of Nyaya-Vaishesika. For the Brahmanical writers it was realism (bahyarthastitva) because it was different from the later, more definite, idealism. But the difference between Sarvastivada and Vijnanavada consists rather in that the former is pluralistic and the latter converts all elements into aspects of one store-consciousness (alaya-vijnana). The whole system of elements is retained with slight variations. O. Rosenberg is inclined to conclude that in theory of cognition the Buddhists were idealists from the beginning, but they were realists so far as they accepted the real existence of a transcendental absolute reality.[194] It has, in any case, a position of its own, very far

---

[192] Samyutta, ii, 94; Majjhim., i, 256 ff.

[193] Mrs. C. Rhys Davids, op. cit., pp. 17 ff., has with very fine discrimination traced the different shades of meaning conveyed in the Pali canonical texts by these terms, which are emphatically declared to be synonymous.

[194] Op. cit., chap. viii.

from ordinary realism, resembling perhaps some modern
theories which accept the reality of external as well as internal
facts and a certain "co-ordination" between them, without the
one "grasping" the other. The cinematographic representation of the world and the converting of all the facts of the inner
and outer world composing an individual stream of life into a
complex play of interconnected momentary flashes, is anything
but realism. The world is a mirage. The reality underlying it is
beyond our cognition. Nagarjuna gave the right explanation
in calling it an empty (shunya) illusion (maya). O.
Rosenberg insists upon the illusionistic tendency of Buddhism
from the very outset.[195] Even for Buddhaghosa not only outer
objects, but men were nothing but puppets trying to deceive
us as to their reality.[196] That Sankara established his
illusionistic doctrine of Vedanta under Buddhist influence is at
present more or less generally accepted. But we must make
the difference between the radical illusionism of Sankara and
Nagarjuna and the half-way illusionism of primitive Buddhism.
The visible world was, as Vachaspatimisra[197] says with reference to Sankhya-Yoga, similar to an illusion, but not exactly
an illusion (mayeva na tu maya). The position of the
Sankhya, accepting the transcendental elements (gunas) as the
only reality, was just the same.

Whether the anatma-dharma theory was the personal crea-
tion of Sakyamuni Buddha himself, or not, is a quite irrelevant
question. In any case, we do not know of any form of Buddhism
without this doctrine and its corrollary classifications of elements into skandha, ayatana, and dhatu, the laws of their
inter-connexion (pratiya-samutpada), and the complicated
constructions which these termini involve. This is also, as

[195] Op. cit., chaps. iv, viii, and xviii.
[196] Visuddhi-magga, xi, Warren, Buddhism, p. 158. Mrs. C. Rhys
Davids, op. cit., denies in primitive Buddhism both illusionism (p. 65)
and idealism (p. 75). When the root of phenomenal existence is declared
to be illusion (avidya), and the process of life is "empty with a twelve-
fold emptiness" (Visuddhi-M., xvii, Warren, op. cit., p. 175), it is difficult
to deny illusionism altogether. As to the different interpretations of
illusion cf. S. Dasgupta, History, p. 384. Professor O. Rosenberg's chief
argument in favour of idealism was drawn from the fact that the objects
of the outer world were components of one samtana, i.e. internal to the
personality. But, considering that in primitive Buddhism all elements
are equally external to one another and samtana is not a reality, not a
dharma, there is no idealism in the later sense. The interpretation
admitted by Mrs. Rhys Davids, p. 75, namely, that "the microcosm (i.e.
pudgala) apprehened the macrocosm by way of its sense-doors," looks
dangerously like satkayadrsti !
[197] Vyasa, iv, 13.

O. Rosenberg rightly remarks, the common foundation of all the forms of Buddhism in all the countries where this religion flourishes at present. Failing to realize that, some superficial observers concluded that in the northern countries Buddhism was "degenerate" and altogether a different religion. It is a salient feature of Indian philosophy that its history splits into several independent lines of development which run parallel from an early beginning down to modern times. Each development has its own fundamental idea to start with, and the development makes every effort to keep faithful to the start. Thus we have the realism (arambha-vada) of the Vaishesika, the pluralism (sanghata-vada) of Buddhism, the evolution (parinama-vada) of Vedanta running in parallel lines of development from the remotest antiquity, each with its own ontology, its own theory of causation, its own theory of cognition, its own idea of salvation, and its own idea of the origin of the limitations (avidya) of our experience.

We know of celebrated philosophers who have been engaged in more than one line, but the lines were always kept separate. In Buddhism the development began in the discussions of the early Hinayana schools. The Sarvastivadins established a catalogue of seventy-five elements. The Sautrantikas excluded a number of them as mere names; the Madhyamikas viewed all of them as contingent (sunya) upon one another, and therefore declared the world to be an illusion; the Vijnanavadins converted them into ideas, aspects of one store-consciousness (alaya-vijnana), but the pluralistic fundamental idea remained; its idealistic and illusionistic tendency, which was clear from the beginning, was elaborately worked out by later scholars.

The possibility is not precluded that the foundation stone of the anatma-dharma theory was laid before Buddha. Just as Mahavira was not the first to proclaim Jainism, but only adopted and gave lustre to a doctrine which existed before him, just so Buddha may have adopted and spread a doctrine which he found somewhere in that philosophical laboratory which was the India of his time. He, indeed, is reported to have emphatically disowned the authorship of a new teaching, but claimed to be the follower of a doctrine established long ago by former Buddhas. This is usually interpreted as a kind of propaganda device, but it is not quite improbable that a real historical fact underlies these assertions.

Among that oldest set of Upanisads which for many reasons are generally admitted to be pre-Buddhistic, but display some knowledge of the Sankhya system, we find, along with Sankhya conceptions, a statement that might be an indication of the existence of such a pre-Buddhistic form of the *anatma-dharma* theory. In the *Kathopanisad*, which belongs to this class, a doctrine is mentioned that is evidently strongly opposed to the monistic view of an immortal soul (*atman*), and favours instead a theory of separate elements (*prthag-dharman pasyati*). This theory is repudiated with the following remark: "Just as rain-water that has fallen down in a desert is scattered and lost among the undulations of the ground, just so is he (philosopher) who maintains the existence of separate elements lost in running after nothing else but these (separate elements)."[198]

Professor H. Jacobi has shown that unorthodox opinions, opposed to the accepted soul-theory, are alluded to even in the oldest set of the Upanisads.[199] These indications are made in the usual Upanisad style and anything but precise.

What emerges from the passage of the *Kathop.* cited above is that there was a doctrine opposed to the reigning soul-theory, that it maintained the existence of subtle elements and separate elements (*prthag dharma*), and that such a doctrine, in the opinion of the author, did not lead to salvation. Sankara, in his commentary, agrees that Buddhism is alluded to, but, very bluntly, he interprets *dharma* as meaning here individual soul.[200] As a matter of fact, *dharma* never occurs with this meaning in the Upanisads. Its occurrence in the *Kathop.* leaves the impression that it is a catchword referring to a foreign and new doctrine, some *anatma-dharma* theory.[201]

---

[198] *Kathop.*, iv, 14; cf. Mrs. and Professor W. Geiger, op. cit., p. 9. In another passage of the same text (i, 21) *dharma* apparently also means an element, but a suitable and immortal one.

[199] Ernst Kuhn Memorial Volume (Munich, 1916), p. 38.

[200] In his commentary on the *Gaudapada Karika*, where the term *dharma* occurs, very clearly in the sense the *Madhyamika* interpretation has given it, namely as something unreal, a mere illusion, the real or the pseudo-Sankara likewise enforces the meaning of an individual soul

[201] There are no traces of the Buddhist meaning of *dharma* having been known to Panini, but there are some traces with regard to its corollary, the term *samskara* or *samskrta*. When causation is to be expressed, he makes a difference between real efficiency, i.e. one fact transgressing its own existence and affecting the other, which he calls *pratiyatna*, explained as *gunantaradhana* (the same as *aticayadhana, paras-paropakara*, or simply, *upakara*,) and an efficiency which is contrasted

Professor Jacobi,[202] in a recent work, arrives at the conclusion that at the epoch of which the Kathop. is the most characteristic exponent the theory of an immortal individual soul was a new idea which, in all probability, enjoyed great popularity as a novelty and met with general approval. There is, indeed, a wide gap between this class of Upanisads and the older set, a difference in style, terminology, and the whole intellectual atmosphere. The idea of a surviving personality, of a Self and even a Universal Self, is not unknown in the Veda: its essence and its relation to Brahma is the main topic of discussion in the Upanisads. But this Self is a psychophysical entity, different explanations of its nature are proposed, and materialistic views are not excluded. The idea of an immortal soul in our sense, a spiritual monad, a simple, uncomposite, eternal, immaterial substance is quite unknown in the Veda, inclusive of the older Upanisads. The new conception was accepted by the Jains, the Sankhyas, Mimamsakas, and later by all philosophical systems except the materialists and the Buddhists. In the Sankhya the old theory survived, in the shape of the *linga-sarira,* along with the adoption of the new.

The attitude of Buddhism towards both the old and the new theories was that of a most emphatic denial. Scholars were always struck by the spirit of extreme animosity which undoubtedly reveals itself in the oldest Buddhist texts whenever the idea of a soul is mentioned. In the light of Professor Jacobi's hypothesis this may find a natural explanation in the feeling of excitement with which the new theory was met and assailed by its chief opponents, for which mere theoretical con-

with it and conceived as two separate facts conditioning one another which he simply calls *samskrta;* it is explained as *sata utkarsadhanam samskarah,* i.e. "a force is what produces (=conditions) an enhancement in (some) extent." In the first case, *upakrta* or *upaskrta* is used, in the second *samskrta,* cf. ii. 3, 53; vi, i. 139; iv, 2, 16; iv, 4, 3; cf., the *Kacika.* That the two *paribhasas, gunantaradhanam* and *sata utkarsadhanam samskarah,* refer to the Sankhya and Buddhist views respectively is probable. In later literature the difference between *upakara* and simple *samskara* is frequently referred to, cf. *Nyayabindutika,* ed. Peterson (*Bibl. Ind.*), p. 13; *dividhaca, sahakari parasparopakari*............: *cf. Six Buddhist Nyaya Tracts,* p. 48 ff.; *Sarvadarshana sangraha,* p. 10 (*Bibl. Ind.*): *sahakarinah kim bhavasya upakurvanti na va.* That the philosophical conceptions involved in this difference were known to Paniui would appear from the suggestive word *pratiyatna=upakara,* as opposed to *samskara,* but this is by no means certain. The conception of *gunantarayoga=vikara* is mentioned in *M. bhasya,* ad v. 1, 2. A similar contrast lies in *adhitya-*versus *pratitya-samutpada,* cf. *Bh. jala-sutta.*

[202] *Die indische Philosophie in Das Licht des Ostens* (Stuttgart, 1922),

siderations of abstract argument seem insufficient to account.
In Buddhist records we find the old and the new soul-theories
clearly distinguished. The doctrine which maintains the
reality of a Self corresponding to the psycho-physical individual
is called *atma-vada*, whereas the view approaching the doctrine
of a permanent Soul is *pudgala-vada*. All Buddhists rejected
the *atma-vada*, since Buddhism (*buddhanucasani*), philo-
sophically, means nothing else than the *dharmata*, the theory
of *dharmas*, which is but another name for *anatman, nairatmya*.
But there are two schools—the Vatsiputriyas and the Sam-
mitiyas—which are, nevertheless, adherents of the *pudgala-vada*.
According to the exposition of Vasubandhu, this means that
the internal *shandhas* at a given moment constitute a certain
unity, which is related to them as fire to fuel.[203] It had not
the absolute reality of a *dharma*, it was not included in the
lists of *dharmas*, but, nevertheless, it was not quite unreal.
This *pudgala* was also regarded as surviving, since it is maintained that it assumes new elements at birth and throws them
off at death.[204]

The *pudgala* of a Buddha seems to be an Omniscient
Eternal Spirit.[205] The *sutra* of the burden-bearer, where
pudgala is compared with the bearer and the *skandhas* with
the burden, was invoked as a proof that Buddha himself
admitted some reality of the *pudgala*.[206] For all the other
Buddhist schools *pudgala* was but another name for *atman*, and
they refuted both theories by the same arguments. That the
position of the Vatsiputriyas was wrong i.e. not in strict conformity with he *dharma*-theory, is evident, since this theory
admits no real unity whatsoever between separate elements.
Threfore Self, Soul, personality, individual, living being,
human being—all these conceptions do not answer to ultimate
realities: they are but names for some combinations of *dharmas*,
i.e. formulas of elements.[207] If our supposition that the *anatma-
dharma* theory is mentioned in the *Kathopanisad* is correct,
it evidently was directed against both the old and the new
Soul-theories as equally unacceptable. But, on the other hand,

---

[203] *Soul Theory*, p. 830.
[204] Ibid., p. 851.
[205] Ibid., p. 841.
[206] Ibid., p. 842. Udyotakara, in his exposition of *atma-vada*
(pp. 338-49), likewise mentions this *sutra* as contradicting the doctrine of
anatman.
[207] Ibid., p. 838.

the tenacious effort of some Buddhist schools to save the idea
of some real unity between the elements of a personal life,[208]
or the idea of a spiritual principle governing it, is partly due
to the difficulty of the problem and partly to an old tradition.
We find, indeed, in the Brahmaṇas and the Upaniṣads something like a forerunner of the Buddhist *skandhas*. The individual is also composed of elements; during his lifetime they
are united; the union ceases at death, and through a reunion of
them a new life begins.[209] Curiously enough, the number of
these elements, or factors, as Professor Jacobi prefers to translate
the term *prana*, is the same as the number of the Buddhist
skandhas.

The elements themselves are quite different, and this
difference bears witness of the enormous progress achieved
by Indian philosophy during the time between the primitive
Upaniṣads and the rise of Buddhism. In the Buddhist system
we have a division of mental faculties into feeling, concept,
will, and pure sensation, in which modern psychology would
not have much to change. In the Upaniṣads it is a very primitive attempt, giving breath, speech, sense of vision, sense of
audition and intellect as the elements. But one point of
similarity remains: the last and, evidently, the most important
element is in both cases *manas*. The macrocosm, or the
Universal Soul, is likewise analysed by the Upaniṣads into five
component elements.[210] In the number of the Buddhist
skandhas and in the position of *manas* (=*vijnana*) among
them we probably have the survival of an old tradition.[211]
It is only by such an indirect influence that we can explain
the astonishing fact of the simultaneous existence of different
classifications of the elements for which there is no intrinsic
requirement in the system. When the *anatma-dharma* theory
was definitely framed, with its theory of causation and theory
of cognition, the classification of elements into "bases" of
cognition (*ayatana*) became quite natural and indispensable,

---

[208] The Sarvastivadins explained the union of the element in a
personality by the operation of a special force (*samskara*), which they
named *prapti*; cf. *supra*, and in the tables of elements in the Appendix II,
where it is found under *viprayukta-samskara* No. 1.

[209] H. Jacobi, op. cit., p. 146. Cf. H. Oldenberg. *Die Weltanschauung
der Brahmana-Texte*, pp. 88, ff., 234.

[210] H. Jacobi, op. cit., p. 146, Cf. H. Oldenberg, *Die Lehre der
Upanishaden*, p. 54.

[211] A similar relation, as is generally admitted, exists between the
three elements *tejas, apas, annam* of the *Chhandogya*, vi, and the three
gunas of the Sankhyas.

but the classification into *skandhas* was useless. It, nevertheless, was retained in compliance with an old habit of thought,
and such changes as were required by the progress of philo-
sophic analysis were introduced.

Thus it is that the fundamental idea of Buddhism—a
plurality of separate elements without real unity—had its roots
in the primitive speculations of the Upanisads. At the time
when a new conception of the Soul was elaborated in
Brahmanical circles, some kind of the pre-Buddhaic Buddhism,
under which we understand the *anatma-dharma* theory, must
have been already in existence. This time is the epoch of the
Kathopanisad, which, as Professor Jacobi points out,[212]
might also be the time of pre-Jinistic Jainism, the time of
Parcvanatha, i.e. the eighth century B.C.

XVI. SUMMARY

To summarize :
The conception of a *dharma* is the central point of the Buddhist
doctrine. In the light of this conception Buddhism discloses
itself as a metaphysical theory developed out of one fundamental principle, *viz.* the idea that existence is an interplay
of a plurality of subtle, ultimate, not further analysable
elements of Matter, Mind, and Forces. These elements are
technically called *dharmas*, a meaning which this word has in
this system alone. Buddhism, accordingly, can be characterized
as a system of Radical Pluralism (*sanghata-vada*)[213]: the elements alone are realities, every combination of them is a mere
name covering a plurality of separate   elements. The moral
teaching of a path towards Final Deliverance is not something
additional or extraneous to this ontological doctrine, it is most
intimately connected with it and, in fact, identical with it.

The connotation of the term *dharma* implies that—

1. Every element is a separate (*prthak*) entity or force.

2. There is no inherence of one element in another,
hence no substance apart from its qualities, no Matter beyond
the separate sense-data, and no Soul beyond the separate
mental data (*dharma=anatman=nirjiva*).

3. Elements have no durtaion, every moment represents
a separate element; thought is evanescent, there are no moving

---

[212] Op. cit., p. 150.
[213] As contrasted with the *arambha-vada*, which maintains the reality
of the whole as well as of the elements, and the *parinama-vada*, which
ascribes absolute reality only to the whole.

bodies, but consecutive appearances, flashings, of new elements in new places (*ksanikatva*).

4. The elements co-operate with one another (*samskrta*).

5. This co-operating activity is controlled by the laws of causation (*pratitya-samutbada*).

6. The world-process is thus a process of co-operation between seventy-two kinds of subtle, evanescent elements, and such is the nature of *dharmas* that they proceed from causes (*hetu-prabhava*) and steer towards extinction (*nirodha*).

7. Influenced (*sasrava*) by the element *avidya*, the process is in full swing. Influenced by the element *prajna*, it has a tendency towards appeasement and final extinction. In the first case streams (*santana*) of combining elements are produced which correspond to ordinary men (*prthag-jana*); in the second the stream represents a saint (*arya*). The complete stoppage of the process of phenomenal life corresponds to a Buddha.

8. Hence the elements are broadly divided into unrest (*duhkha*), cause of unrest (*duhkha-samudaya=avidya*), extinction (*nirodha*), and cause of extinction (*marga=prajna*).

9. The final result of the world-process is its suppression. Absolute Calm : all co-operation is extinct and ·replaced by immutability (*asamskrta=nirvana*).

Since all these particular doctrines are logically developed out of one fundamental principle, Buddhism can be resolved in a series of equations:

dharmata=natratmya=ksanikatva=samskrtatva=pratity-smmutpannatva =, sasrava-anasravatva=samkleca-vyavadanatva =duhkha-nirodha=samsara-nirvana. ...

But, although the conception of an element of existence has given rise to an imposing superstructure in the shape of a consistent system of philosophy, its inmost nature remains a riddle. What is *dharma*? It is inconceivable! It is subtle! No one will ever be able to tell what its real nature (*dharma-svabhava*) is! It is transcendental!

APPENDIX I

VASUBANDHU ON THE FUNDAMENTAL PRINCIPLE OF THE SARVASTIVADA SCHOOL

The fifth chapter (*kosha-sthana*) of the *Abhidharma-kosha* (v, 24-6) contains a detailed exposition of the argument between the Sarvasivadins or Vaibhasikas and the Sautrantikas upon the question of the reality of future and past elements (*dharmas*), written according to the method of later dialectics. It is divided in two parts, *purvapaksa* and *uttarapaksa*. In the first the Vaibhasika makes a statement of his case, and he is attacked by the Sautrantika; he answers the questions and triumphs over the opponent. In the second the parts are reversed: the Vaibhasika puts the questions and the Sautrantika answers them and secures the final victory. As a conclusion the Vaibhasika gives voice to his despair at the impossibility of conceiving the transcendentally deep essence of the elements of existence. The translation is made from the Tibetan text of the Peking edition of the Bstanhgyur, Mdo, vol. 64, fol. 279, b. 5-285, a. 2. Some explanations have been introduced from Yashomitra's Commentary, and the Tibetan commentary of Mchims-pa, which is the standard work for *abhidharma* throughout Mongolia and Tibet.

AN EPISODICAL INVESTIGATION INTO THE POSSIBILITY OF PAST AND FUTURE EFFICIENCY

(*Abhidharma-kosha, Karikas* V, 24-6)

(The author establishes that some passions exist only at the time when the corresponding objects are present, such are love or disgust towards sense-objects. But there are other passions of a general scope, such as preconceived dogmatical ideas, delusions, a doubting turn of mind, etc.; these have a bearing towards all objects whether past, present or future. The following question is then raised).

BSTAN-HGYUR, 64, f. 279, b. 5.

But are this past and this future really existent or not? If they are, it would follow that the elementary forces (*samskara*) (which are active in the process of life) must be permanent (i.e immovable), since they exist through all time. If they are not, how is it to be explained that a man is attracted to (objects past and future) by such (passion as he experienced formerly, or will be subject to in future)?

The *Vaibhasikas* do not admit those elements (which combine in the process of life) to be permanent, since they are subject (to the action of four energies which are) the characteristic appurtenance of such elements (*viz.* the forces of origination, decay, existence, and destruction). But, on the other hand, they emphatically declare that "the times" (i.e. everyone of the three times) are existent in reality.

The *Sautrantika* asks, for what reason?

(Part I—*The case for Everlasting Elements*)

KARIKA, v, 24.

The *Vaibhasika answers*: The times are always existent (1) because this has been declared in Scripture, (2) because of the double (cause of perception), (3) because of the existence of the perception's object, (4) because of the production of a result (by previous deeds). Since we maintain that all this exists, we profess the theory that everything exists (*Sarvastivada*).

279, b. 7.

YACOM

(1) *Because this has been declared in Scripture*.—Our Sublime Lord has declared: ("the elements of matter. O Brethren, the past and the future ones, are impermanent, not to speak of the present ones. This is perceived by the perfect saint, endowed, as he is, with wisdom. Therefore, he is regardless of past sense-objects, he does not rejoice at future enjoyments, he entertains disgust and aversion in regard to the present ones, he is engaged in keeping them off).

279, b. 7

O Brethren! if some kind of past matter did not exist, the perfect saint endowed with wisdom could not be regardless of past sense-objects, but, since they are existent, he (enjoys the privilege of) disregarding them. If some kind of future matter were not existent, the wise and perfect saint could not be free from rejoicing at future enjoyments .(since his independence would have no object). But future sense-objects do exist, etc."

5

280, a. 2

(2) *Because of the double (cause of perception)*—It is declared in Scripture: "consciousness, when operating, is conditioned by (elements) of a double kind." What are they? The sense of vision and colour (for a visual consciousness), and so (on an organ cf perception and its respective object for each of the six kinds of consciousness, the last being) the intellect itself and its non-sensuous objects[1], (for consciousness purely mental).

Thus these first two reasons for admitting the existence of the past and the future are taken from Scripture, but there are others, too, which are founded on argument.

280, a 4

(3) *Because of the existence of an object.*—If there is an object, its cognition can arise; if there is none, neither can its cognition be produced. If the past and the future were not existent, the objects (of the corresponding cognition) would be non-existent, they could not be cognized.

YACOM

(4) *Because of the production of a result (by former deeds).*— If the past did not exist, how could a deed, good or bad, attain, after some lapse of time, its fruition, since, at the time when the latter appears, the cause which has produced retribution is gone. (A former deed, good or bad, does exist in reality, because, when it becomes ripe, it produces fruition, just as a present one does).

280, a. 6

For these reasons we *Vaibhasikas* maintain that the past and the future necessarily exist. This leads to the theory that everything is existent, and our school is known by emphatically adhering to the principle of such universal existence (*Sarvastivada*). Accordingly (it is said above in the moemonic verse): "since we maintain that all this exists, we profess the theory that everything exists." Those who maintain that everything, past, future and present, exists are advocates of universal existence (*Sarvastivadins*). On the other hand, those who make a distinction, partly admitting and partly denying this theory, are termed the Distinguishing School (*Vibhajya-*

---

[1] *Manah and dharmah.*

vadins). They maintain that the present elements, and those among the past that have not yet produced their fruitions, are existent, but they deny the existence of the future ones and of those among the past that have already produced fruition.[2]

280₁ b. 2

Sautrantika.—And how many branches are there among these advocates of universal existence ?

KARIKA, v, 25

Vaibhasika.—There are four branches, inasmuch as they maintain (1) a -change of existence (*bhava-parinama*), (2) a change of aspect (*laksana-parinama*), (3) a change of condition (*avastha-parinama*), or (4) contingency (*apeksa-parinama*). The third is all right. The difference in time reposes on a difference of condition (i.e. function of the elements).

280₂ b. 3.

(1) It was the venerable Dharmatrata who maintained the view that existence (*bhava*) changes in the course of time, not substance (*dravya*). He is known to have been arguing thus: when an element enters different times, its existence changes, but not its essence, just as when a golden vessel is broken, its form changes, but not its colour. And when milk is turned into curds, its taste, consistency, and digestive value are gone, but not its colour.[3] In the same manner, when an element, after having been future, enters into a present time, it gets rid of its future existence, but not of the existence of its essence, and when from present it becomes past, it casts away its present existence, but not the existence of its substance.

280₃ b. 6.

(8) It was the venerable Ghosa who assumed a change in the aspect of the elements (*laksana*). He is known to have professed the theory that, when an element appears at different times, the past one retains its past aspect, without being severed from its future and present aspects, the future has its future aspect, without being altogether deprived of its past and present aspects, the present likewise retains its present aspect, without completely losing its past and future aspects. Just as, when a man falls into passionate love with a female, he is not

---

[2] Cf. above, p. 36.
[3] Or, if *rupa* stands for *svarupa*, "its essence."

altogether deprived of his capacity of love towards other females (but this capacity is not prominent).

281, a. 1.

YACOM

(3) A change of condition (*avastha*) is advocated by the venerable Vasumitra. He is known to have maintained that, when one element manifests itself at different times, it changes in condition and receives different designations according to the condition which it has reached, without changing in substance. (When an element is in a condition in which it does not yet produce its function, it is called future; when it produces it, it is called present; when, having produced it, it ceases to wrok, it is past, its substance remaining the same). Just as in an abacus the same ball receives different significations according to the place it is thrown in. If it is thrown in the place for units it means one, if in the place for hundreds it means a hundred, if in the place for thousands it means one thousand.

281, a. 3.

YACOM

(4) An advocate of contingency (*apeksa*) is the venerable Buddhadeva. He is known to have maintained the principle that an element in the course of time receives this or that denomination on account of its relation to the former and the next moment. (An element is future with respect to the former one, be it past or present, it is present with respect to a former, i.e. past one, or with respect to the next one, i.e. future one, it is past with respect to the next one, be it present or future). Just as the same female may be called a mother (with respect to her children) and a daughter (with respect to her own mother).

Thus it is that all these four (lines of thought) are so many varieties of the theory which maintains Universal Existence. As regards the first of them, it is nothing else than the doctrine of the changing manifestations (of one eternal matter). Therefore it must be included in the Sankhya system (which has already been rejected). As to the second, it is a confusion of all times, since it implies co-existence of all the aspects (of an element) at the same time. The passion of a man may be prominent towards one female, and merely existent (imperceptibly) towards another one, but what has this fact to do with the theory it is supposed to illustrate? According to the fourth explanation, it would follow that all the three times are found together, included in one of them. Thus in the scope of the past time we can distinguish a former and a following moment. They will represent a past and a future time. Between them the intermediate moment will correspond to a present time.

281, a. 7.

Thus it is that among all proposed explanations the (remaining one alone), the third in number, is right, that which maintains a change of condition (or function). According thereto the difference in time reposes on the difference in function: at the time when an element does not yet actually perform its function it is future; when performing it, it becomes present; when, after having performed it, it stops, it becomes past:

281, b. 1.

Sautrantika—Although I perfectly understand all this, I do not see my way to admit that it implies a real existence of the past and of the future. For, if the past is really -existent and the future likewise, what induces us (to make a distinction between them and) to call them past and future?

Vaibhasika—But have we not already explained it: the time of an element is settled in accordance with the time of its function.

Sautrantika—If this be the case, an eye which does not look at the present moment will not be present, because it does not perform its function?

Vaibhasika—It is present (because it performs its other functions) : it is the immediate cause (of the next moment of its existence and the remote cause) determining (its future character).

MCHIMS—*pa, ii, 166, a. 4*

(Although an eye that does not look is not performing its function, it, nevertheless, is efficient in immediately producing and forecasting the homogeneousness of its future with its past and in producing its, so-called, co-operative result.[4] In that sense it is present).

---

[4] The Sarvastivadins establish several kinds of causal relations between the elements. If e.g. a moment of the sense of vision produces in the

Sautrantika—In that case the past will be the same as the present, since the past likewise produces such results—the past viewed as a cause of homogeneousness in consecutive moments,[5] as a general moral cause,[6] and as a cause requiring retribution[7] —all these causes would be present since they may perform their actual functions at the present moment.

Vaibhasika—I call present a cause which exhibits at the present moment a double function—that of giving an immediate result and that of determining the character of its remote future. A past cause, although it may produce a result at the present moment, does not, at present, determine its general character (which has been previously determined). Therefore the past is not the same as the present.

Sautrantika—If the time is settled according to efficiency, an element may be past inasmuch as its power of determining the general character of a remote result belongs to the past, and it may be present nevertheless, since it produces the result of the present moment. Thus a confusion of the characteristic signs of all the three times will arise, and I maintain that you are guilty of such confusion.

281, b. 3.

Your standpoint leads to the absurdity of assuming actual or semi-actual past causes (i.e. semi-present elements), since the cause of homogeneousness and other past causes may produce a (present) result. A confusion of the essential natures of the three times is the consequence.

---

next moment a visual sensation, it is termed *karana-hetu* and its result *adhipati-phala*. This relation will be absent in the case of an inefficient condition of the organ of vision. But there are other relations between the moments of this organ. When the next moment is just the same as the foregoing one, thus evoking in the observer the idea of duration, this relation is termed *sabhaga-hetu* as to a *nisyanda-phala*. If this moment appears in a stream (*santana*) which is defiled by the presence of passions (*klesha*), this defiling character is inherited by the next moments, if no stopping of it is produced. Such a relation is called *sarvatraya-hetu* as to *nisyanda-phala*. Finally every moment in a stream is under the influence of former deeds (*karma*) and may, in its turn, have an influence on future events. This relation is termed *vipaka-hetu* as to *vipaka-phala*. The simultaneity of the inseparable elements of matter will produce a cooperative result (*purusakara-phala*). These last three relations must be existent even in the case of a non-operative moment of the sense of vision. Cf. *Ab. K.*, ii. 50 ff.; O. Rosenberg, *Problems*, chap. xv.

[5] *Sabhaga-hetu.*
[6] *Sarvatraga-hetu.*   [7] *Vipaka-hetu.*

(PART II. THE CASE AGAINST EVERLASTING ELEMENTS)

281, b. 4.

KARIKA, v, 25.

Sautrantika—To this we must make the following reply: What is it that keeps (an element from exhibiting its ction)? And how is (the time of this action to be determined)? If it. the time of an element's existence, does not differ from the essence of the element itself, there will altogether be no time. If the element in the future and in the past exists just in the same sense as in the present, why is it future and past? The essence of the elements of existence (*dharmata*) is deep!

281, b. 4.

If the essence alone of the elements of existence persists throughout all the three times, but not their function, what is it that constitutes an implement to this function? What is it that sometimes induces them to perform and sometimes keeps them back from performing their function?

Vaibhasika—The function is performed when all the necessary conditions are present.

Sautrantika—This won't do! because (according to your theory) tnese conditions are always present. Again, as to the functions themselves, they likewise may be past, future, and present. They then require an explanation in their turn.

281, b. 6.

Will you admit the existence of a second function (which will determine the time of the first)? or will you suppose that it neither is past, nor future, nor present, but that it, nevertheless, does exist? In this case this function will not be subject to the elementary forces of life (*samskrta*) and will represent an immovable eternal entity (*asamskrta*). For this reason you cannot maintain that. as long as an element does not yet perform its function, it is future.

281, b. 7.

Baibhasika—If the function of an element were something different from the element itself, your objections would be right. But since it is not different they do not hold good.

Sautrantika—Then there is no time at all! If the function is the same as the substance, the elements will always remain identical. For what reason are they sometimes called past, sometimes future, and sometimes present?

Vaibhasika—An element that has not yet appeared is future, one which has appeared and not disappeared is present, one which has disappeared is past. What is it you find unfounded in this explanation?

Sautrantika—The following point needs here to be established:

If the past and the future exist in the same sense as the present, as realities, why is it, then, that, being existent in the same sense, they are future and past? If the substance of the same element is alone (permanently) existent, what is the reason that it is spoken of as "having not yet appeared" or "gone"? What is it that does not appear later on and whose absence makes us call it past"?

Thus it is that the notion of three times will altogether have no real foundation, as long as you don't accept the view that the elements appear into life out of non-existence and return again into non-existence after having been existing. (Your theory implies eternal existence of the elements).

Vaibhasika—It is absurd to maintain that it implies eternal existence! There are the four forces (of origination, decay, maintainance, and destruction) to which every element is subject, and the combination (of the permanent essence of an element with these forces produces its impermanent manifestations in life).

Sautrantika—Mere words! They cannot explain the origination and decay (which are going on in the process of life). An element, according to this view, is permanent and impermanent at the same time. This, indeed, is something quite new! It has been said on this occasion:

282, a. 7.

Maintained eternal essence;
Denied eternal being!
And yet no difference between
This essence and this being.
'Tis clearly a caprice
Of the Almighty!
'Tis spoken by His order!

(*Vaibhasika*—But Buddha has said that there "is" a past and there "is" a future).

Sautrantika—We, likewise, maintain that there "is" a past and there "is" a future. But this means that what has been formerly "is" past, and what, in the (presence of its causes), will happen "is" future. They exist in this sense only, in reality.

282, b. 1.

Vaibhasika—Who has ever maintained that they exist just in the same sense in which the present exists ?

Sautrantika—How can one exist otherwise ?

Vaibhasika—The essence of the past and of the future is (always) existent.

Sautrantika—If they are always existent, how is the (remarkable result) brought about that they are called past or future? Therefore the words of our Sublime Lord, "there is a past, there is a future," must be understood in another sense. He proffered them when discussing with the Ajivikas (who denied moral responsibility for past deeds). He strongly opposed their doctrine, which denied the connexion between a past cause and a future result. In order to make it known that a former cause and a future are something which happened formerly and will happen in future, he categorically declared : "There is a past, there is a future." For the word "is" acts as a particle (which may refer to something existent and to non-existence as well). As e.g. people will say: "there is absence of light" (before it has been kindled), "there is absence of light after (it has been put out)," or the "light is put out, but I did not put it out." When Buddha declared that there "is" a past and there "is" a future, he used the word "is" in that sense. Had it been otherwise, it would be absolutely impossible to account for (the notions of) a past and a future.

282, b. 5.

Vaibhasika—But, then, how are we to understand the words of our Sublime Lord when addressing the Lagudacikhi-yaka wandering ascetics (the bearers of a tress on the head and a stick in the hand) ? Why did he declare: "a deed (which requires immediate retribution) is past, is accomplished, is finished, is gone, has disappeared, but, nevertheless, it does exist." What did these ascetics really deny ? Not that the accomplished deed was past, (but that it could have some actual existence, i.e. some efficiency. Hence the words of Buddha imply an actual existence of the past).

282, b. 7.

Sautrantika—(No!) He meant that a force to produce retribution is driven by a past deed into the run (of combined elements which constitute an individual). Were it existent in reality, it would not be past. This is the only way in which this passage needs be understood, because on another occasion, in the sermon about "Non-substantiality as the Ultimate Truth",[8] the sublime Lord has spoken thus: "when the organ of vision appears into life, there is absolutely nothing from which it proceeds, and when it vanishes, nought there is to which it retires. Therefore, O Brethren, this organ of vision has no former existence. Then it appears, and after having been existent it vanishes again." If a future organ of vision were existent, Buddha would never have declared that it appeared out of non-existence (out of nothing).

283, a. 2.

Vaibhasika—(This passage means that), as far as the present time is concerned, it did not exist and then appeared (in the scope of this time).

Sautrantika—Impossible ! Time is not something different from the object (existing in it).

Vaibhasika—But may not its essence have not been present and then have appeared ?

Sautrantika—This would only prove that it had no (real) future existence.

(The second argument of the Sarvastivadins refuted)

283. a. 3.

Sautrantika—Now your second argument is drawn from the circumstance that cognition, when arising, reposes on two factors: a perceptive faculty and a corresponding object. Here we must at first (consider the instance) of mental cognition reposing on the operation of the intellect and on a mental (not sensuous) object.[9] Is this object a real cause in the same sense as the intellect? or is it a mere (passive) object realized by the intellect? If it were a real active cause, how could events which must happen after the lapse of a thousand

---

[8] *Paramartha-sunyata-sutra*, Samyuktagama, xiii, 22 (McGovern).
[9] *dharmah*, i.e., 64 *dharmas*, *ayatana* No. 12.

æons, or those which never will happen, possibly constitute
an active cause of the corresponding cognition? And the
Final Deliverance, which is synonymous with the total
cessation of every operation of all the elements of existence,
how can it constitute a really active cause of its own conception? But if, on the other hand, such objects are mere
passive objects of the operating mind, then I maintain that
they may be future and may be past.

283, a. 7.

Vaibhasika—If they altogether do not exist, how can they
possibly be objects?

Sautrantika—Their existence I admit, (understanding by
existence) that very form in which they are conceived by us at
the present moment in the present place.

281, a, 8.

Vaibhasika—And how are they conceived?

Sautrantika—As past and as future. If somebody remem-
bers a past object or a former feeling, he has never been
observed to say "it exists", but only, "it did exist."

(*The third argument of the Sarvastivadins examined*)

283, b. 1.

Sautrantika—As (to the cognition of past and future) sense
objects, the past ones are remembered in that very form in
which they were experienced when they were present, and
the future ones are known to Buddhas just in that form in
which they will appear at the time when they will be present.

Vaibhasika—And if it be just the same existence (as the
present one)?

Sautrantika—Then it is present.

Vaibhasika—If not?

Sautrantika—(It is absent: and thus) it is proved that
absence can be cognized just as well (as presence).

Vaibhasika—But (will you not admit that the past and
the future) are fragments of the present itself?

Sautrantika—No, because we are not conscious of
apprehending fragments.

Vaibhasika—But, then, it may represent the same stuff,
with the mere (difference that in the past and the future) its
atoms may be disjoined?

Sautrantika—In that case, atoms will be eternally existent,

and (all the process of life) will consist in their either combining or disjoining. There will altogether be no new origination, no real extinction, and thus you will become guilty of
adhering to the (heretical) doctrine of the Ajivikas.

283, b. 4.

Moreover, you will be contradicted by the scriptural passage
(referred to above) : "when the organ of vision is produced, it
does not come from some other place ; when it disappears, it
is not going to be stored up in another place, etc."

On the other hand, it is impossible that feelings and other
(mental phenomena), which have no atomic structure, should
be divided into fragments. If remembered, they likewise are
remembered in that very form in which they did appear and
were experienced. And, if you suppose that they continue to
exist in the same form, they must be eternal. If they do not,
it will be proved that (a non-existent feeling) may be apprehended (by memory) just as well (as an existent one is apprehended by self-perception).

283, b. 6.

Vaibhasika—If non-existence is capable of being apprehended, you must add to (the list of all things cognizable, i.e.)
to the twelve bases of cognition (*ayatana*), a new category, the
thirteenth, non-existence.

Sautrantika—Supposing I think about the absence of a
thirteenth category, what will be then the object corresponding
to my thought ?

Vaibhasika—It will be this very (category, i.e. its) name.

Sautrantika—And what is it (generally speaking) that we
apprehend, when we are expecting to hear a word which as
yet is not pronounced ?

Vaibhasika—It is nothing else than this very word.

Sautrantika—Then a person who desires not to hear this
word, will be obliged to pronounce it !

Vaibhasika—It may be the future condition of this word ?

Sautrantika—If it is something existent, why does it
produce an idea of absence ?

Vaibhasika—There it may be its present absence.

Sautrantika—No! it is the same. (If this present absence
is something existent, why does it produce an idea of non-
existence ?)

Vaibhasika—Then it may be the characteristic sign of a future; (this sign is absent at present, and gives rise to the idea of non-existence).

Sautrantika—This sign consists (in the fact that the future) will appear into existence out of a previous non-existence. Thus it is that both existence and non-existence may be objects of cognition.

284, a. 2.

Vaibhasika—And how do you explain the words of the future Buddha. who has spoken thus : "that these persons know or perceive things which do not exist in the world—this is impossible !" ?

Sautrantika—These words (do not mean that non-existence cannot be an object of cognition, but they) have the following meaning :—"there are other, manifestly deluded, persons (who have not yet attained the divine power of vision : they) perceive things that never did exist. I perceive only existing (remote) things." If, on the contrary, every possible thought had only existing things for its object, what reason could there have been for doubting (the accuracy of the assertion of such people about what they were perceiving by their power of divine vision) ? or what would have been the difference (between the *bodhisattva's* real power of vision and the incomplete power of these men) ?

284, a. 5.

It is inevitable that we should understand the passage in this sense, because it is confirmed by another scriptural passage. which begins with the words : " 'come unto me, ye monks, my pupils !' and goes on until the following words are spoken : "what I am telling him in the morning becomes clearer at night, what I am conversing about at night becomes clearer to him next morning. He will cognize the existence of what does exist. the non-existence of what does not exist. Where something still higher exists, he will know that there is something still higher ; and where nothing higher exists, he will know that (it is the Final Deliverance, that) there is nothing higher than that !" Therefore the argument (in favour of a real existence of the past, that you have drawn from the supposed fact that) our intellect can have only existent things for its object—this argument is wrong.

(The fourth argument of the Sarvastivadins examined)
284, a. 7.

Sautrantika—As to your next argument (in favour of the real existence of the past, viz., because it has a real) result, we must observe that we, the Sautrantikas, never did maintain that a result can be produced from a past deed (directly).

Vaibhasika—How is it produced, then?

Sautrantika—(This deed) is the beginning of a peculiar chain of events (in the course of which the result appears sooner or later). A more detailed explanation of this point will be given later on, when we will refute the theory (of the Vatsiputriyas, who) maintain the existence of an individual.[10] (As to your view, it is manifestly inconsistent), What result can a past deed produce according to this view? If the past and the future are actually existent, the result will necessarily be pre-existent from all eternity.

Vaibhasika—(But we assume the existence of the force of generation ?)

284, b. 1.

Sautrantika—Well, then, it will be established that this force itself appears after having previously been no-existent ! In fact, if everything without any exception is pre-existent, there can be nothing that could have a force to produce any-thing! In the end it comes to the same as the theory of the followers of Varsaganya. According to them there is neither production of something new nor extinction of something existent: what exists is always existent, what does not exist will never become existent.

Vaibhasika—But the force (of a past deed) may consist in "making present" (some already existing element)?

284, b. 3.

Sautrantika—How is this "making present" to be under-stood ?

Vaibhasika—It consists in removing (the result from one) place to another.

Sautrantika—Then the result would be eternally pre-existent. And, as to non-existent elements, how can they (be made to change place)? Moreover, such "removing" means production (of a motion, i.e. of something) which previously did not exist.

[10] *Ab. K.*, ix, translated in my *Soul Theory*.

284, b. 5.

Vaibhasika—It may consist in a "specification" of the (ever-lasting) essence of an element?

Sautrantika—This, agian, would prove that there is production of what previously did not exist. To conclude: the principle of Universal Existence, as far as exegetical literature is concerned, where is implies an actual existence of the past and of the future, does not hold good. On the contrary, it is all right if we strictly conform to the words of Scripture, where it is declared that "everything exists."

Vaibhasika—And in what sense has it been declared in Scripture that "everything exists"?

Sautrantika—O Brahmins! it has been declared, "everything exists": that means no more than "the elements included in he twelve categories (*ayatana*) are existent."

Vaibhasika—And the three times (are they not included among these elements)?

Sautrantika—(No, they are not!) How their existence is to be understood we have already explained:

(*The Sarvastivadin reverts to his first argument*)

284, b. 7.

Vaibhasika—If the past and the future did not exist, how could it be possible that a man should be attracted by (a past and future passion) to a (past or future object of enjoyment)?

Sautrantika—This becomes possible because past passions leave residues (or produce seeds), which are the causes of new passions; these seeds are existent (and the saint has the capacity of keeping them down, of being independent of them). Therefore, a man can be bound by (past accesses of) passion. And it is in this sense that he can be allured by (future or past) objects, because the seeds of these passions, which are directed towards (past and future enjoyments), are always present in him.

Conclusion

Cf. Mchims-pa, ii, 167, b. 7. 285, a. 1.

Vaibhasika (does not feel discountenanced by this series of arguments, and says:) We Vaibhasikas, nevertheless, maintain that the past and the future certainly do exist. But (regarding the everlasting essence of the elements of existence, we confess) that this is something we do not succeed in explaining, their essence is deep (it is transcendental), since its existence cannot be established by rational methods.[11] (And as to the use we make of the notion of time in common life, it is contradictory. We use) the expression: "what appears vanishes" (implying that the same element appears and disappears, e.g.) "some matter appears and disappears". But we, likewise, say "one thing appears, another disappears," implying that one element, the future one, enters into life, and another one (the present one) stops. We also speak of the appearing of time (itself "the time is come"), because the element which enters into life is included in the notion of time. And we speak about being born "from time", since the future includes many moments (and only one of them actually enters into life).

End of the Episodical Investigation

APPENDIX II

TABLE OF THE ELEMENTS ACCORDING TO THE SARVASTIVADINS
GENERAL VIEW

All elements of existence (*sarvam* = 75 *dharmas*)

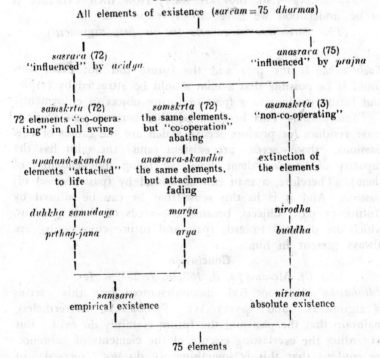

sasrava (72) "influenced" by *avidya*		*anasrava* (75) "influenced" by *prajna*
samskrta (72) 72 elements "co-operating" in full swing	*samskrta* (72) the same elements, but "co-operation" abating	*asamskrta* (3) "non-co-operating"
upadana-skandha elements "attached" to life	*anasrava-skandha* the same elements, but attachment fading	extinction of the elements
duhkha samudaya	*marga*	*nirodha*
prthag-jana	*arya*	*buddha*
samsara empirical existence		*nirvana* absolute existence

75 elements

[11] The Peking and Narthang Bstan-hgyur read here *dran-bar mi nus-so*. This may mean that the remark of the Vaibhasika applies to the

CLASSIFICATION OF ALL ELEMENTS OF EXISTENCE

(Sarvam=anatman=12 ayatanas=18 dhatus=75 dharmas)

I. First General Division

1. Samskrta......co-operating, impermanent......72 dharmas
2. Asamskrta—non-co-operating, immutable...... 3   „

II. Second General Division

1. susrava......"influenced" by passions, process of life in full
swing.
2. anasrava...... 'uninfluenced" by passions, process of life
abating and suppressed.

The first item corresponds to the seventy-two sanskrta-
dharmas as far as they co-operate in the production of an ordinary life (prthag-jana), the second contains the three eternal
elements (asamskrta) and the samskrta as well, in those cases
when life is being gradually suppressed and the individual
becomes a saint (arya).

III. Third General Division, into four stages (satya)

1. dukha......unrest   ⎫
2. samudaya......its cause ⎬ =the 72 sasrava-dharma.
                              ⎭
3. nirodha...eternal peace=the 3 asamskrta ⎫ anasrava-
4. marga......its cause=the remaining anasrava ⎬ dharma
                                              ⎭

IV. Fourth General Division

from the view-point of the part played by the elements in the
process of cognition, into six subjective and six objective
"bases" (ayatana) of cognition.

I. Six internal bases (adhyatma-ayatana) or -receptive faculties (indriya).	II. Six external bases (bahya-ayatana) or objects (visaya).
1. Sense of vision (caksur indriya-ayatana).	7. Colour and shape (rupaayatana)..
2. Sense of audition (crotratindriya ayatana).	8. Sound (cabda-ayatana).
3. Sense of smelling (ghrana-indriya-ayatana).	9. Odour (gandha-ayatana).

elements of mind alone, i.e. the elements that cannot be carried from one
place to another, But Sanghabhadra's text points to a reading bçad-par
mi nus-so, which undoubtedly is the correct one, since it is supported by
the translation of Hiuen-Tsang. The corruption must be very old, since
the block-print of the Aga monastery. which is founded on old sources
coming from Derge, repeats it and it is retained by Mchims-pa.

(Internal Bases)	(External Bases)
4. Sense of taste (*jihva-in-driya-ayatana*).	10. Taste (*rasa-ayatana*).
5. Sense of touch (*kaya-in-driya-ayatana*).	11. Tangibles (*sprastavya-ayatana*).
6. Faculty of the intellect or consciousness (*mana-indriya-ayatana*).	12. Non-sensuous objects (*dharma-ayatana* or *dharmah*).

In this classification the eleven first items correspond to eleven (*dharma*), each including one. The twelfth item contains all the remaining sixty-four elements, and it is therefore called *dharma-ayatana* or simply *dharmah*, i.e. the remaining elements.

V. *Fifth General Division*

into eighteen classes (*dhatu=gotra*) of elements represented in the composition of an individual stream of life (*santana*) in the different planes of existence.

I. Six *indriyas*.	II. Six *visayas*.
1. *caksur-dhatu*, sense of vision.	7. *rupa-dhatu*, colour.
2. *crotra-dhatu*, „ „ audition.	8. *cabda-dhatu*, sound.
3. *ghrana-dhatut*, „ „ smelling.	9. *gandha-dhatu*, odour.
	10. *rasa-dhatu*, taste.
4. *jihva-dhatu*, „ „ taste.	11. *sprastavya-dhatu*, tangible.
5. *kaya-dhatu*, „ „ touch.	
	12. *dharma-dhatu*, or *dhar-mah*, non-sensuo objects.
6. *mano-dhatu*, „ „ faculty of intellect.	

III. Six *vijñanas*.

13. Visual consciousness	(*caksur-vijñana-dhatu*)
14. Auditory „	(*shrotra-vijñana-dhatu*)
15. Olfactory „	(*ghrana-vijñana-dhatu*)
16. Gustatory „	(*jihva-vijñana-dhatu*)
17. Tactile „	(*kaya-vijñana-dhatu*)
18. Non-sensuous „	(*mano-vijñana-dhatu*)

Ten of these *dhatus* contain one dharma each (Nos. 1-5 and 6-11); the *dhatu* No. 12 contain sixty-four *dharmas* (forty-six *caitta*, fourteen *citta-viprayukta*, three *asamskrta*, and avi-

jñapti) consciousness, representing a single *dharma*, is split into seven *dhatus*, No. 6 and Nos. 13-18.

On the sensuous plane of existence (*kama-Dhatu*) the individual streams (*santana*) are composed of all the eighteen *dhatus*. In the world of "Reduced Matter" (*rupa-Dhatu*) the *dhatus* Nos. 9-10 and 15-16 are absent, and the individuals are composed of only fourteen *dhatus*. In the Immaterial Worlds (*arupa-Dhatu*) they are composed of only three *dhatus*, Nos. 6, 12 and 18, since all matter and sensuous consciousness does not exist there.

The six *visayas* are *visaya* in regard to the six *indriyas*, but *alambana* in regard to the six *vijnanas*.

VI *Sixth division*, of the seventy-two active elements (*samskrta-dharma*) into five groups (*skandha*).

1. *rupa-skandha*	...	the physical elements, matter	11 dharmas
2. *vedana-skandha*	..	feeling	1 dharma
3. *sanjna-skandha*	...	conception	1 dharma
4. *samskara-skandha*	..	will and other forces	58 dharmas
5. *vijnana-skandha*	...	pure consciousness (without content)	1 dharma
		Together	72 dharmas

Group means collection, *viz.*, of *dharmas* past, present and future, remote and near, pure and defiled, etc. The *asamskrta* are not included in this division, but the other *anasrava*, as well as the *sasrava*, are included. When the *sasrava* alone are meant, the groups are called *upadana-skandha*, i.e. elements of "attachment" to life : Other synonyms are *rana* "struggle", *duhkha* "unrest" *duhkha-samudaya* "cause of unrest" *loka* "mundane existence", *drsti-sthiti* "the place where the belief in the existence of personality obtains", *bhava* "existence" simply, since by existence simply the usual existence of ordinary men is meant.

When the *skandhas* embrace all the *samskrta-dharmas*, the *sasrava* and *anasrava* as well, they receive, in contra-distinction to the *upadana-skandhas*, other names : *adhvanah* "the (three) times". *katha-vastu* "objects of speech", *saniksarana* "elements to be suppressed", *savastuka* "having empirical reality", or "being subject to causality". The *skandha* No. 4 contains all the *caitta-dharmas*, except *vedana* and *sanjna*, i.e. forty-four mental faculties with *cetana*, the will as the principal one, and fourteen general forces (*citta-viprayukta*).

THE SINGLE ELEMENTS OF MATTER (RUPA), MIND (CITTA-CAITTA), FORCES (VIPRAYUKTA-SAMSKARA), AND ETERNITY (ASAMSKRTA)

A. MATTER (Rupa)

1. *caksur-indriya*, translucent matter (*rupa-prasada*) conveying visual sensations.
2. *crotra-indriya*, translucent matter (*rupa-prasada*) conveying auditory sensations.
3. *ghrana-indriya*, translucent matter (*rupa-prasada*) conveying olfactory sensations.
4. *jihva-indriya*, translucent matter (*rupa-prasada*) conveying taste sensations.
5. *kaya-indriya*, translucent matter (*rupa prasada*) conveying tactile sensations.
6. *rupa-visaya*, visual sense-data.
7. *shabda-visaya*, auditory sense-data.
8. *gandha-visaya*, olfactory sense-data.
9. *rasa-visaya*, taste sense-data.
10. *sprastavya-visaya*, tactile sense-data.
11. *avijnapti*, unmanifested matter, the vehicle of moral qualities.

Matter is divided into primary (*bhuta=mahabhuta*) and secondary (*bhautika*). Four atoms of primary matter, one from each *mahabhuta*, are necessary to support one *bhautika-atom*. Only No. 10, the tactile class, contains both all the primary and some secondary kinds of tactibility: all the other classes contain only secondary, supported, kind of matter.

The Four Universal Elements of Matter (*mahabhut(a)*)

1. *prthivi*, element manifesting itself as hard-stuff, or repulsion.
2. *ap*,   ,,   ,,   ,,   viscous-stuff or attraction
3. *tejas*,   ,,   ,,   ,,   heat-stuff
4. *irana*   ,,   ,,   ,,   motion-stuff

Avijñapti is a variety of *karma*. Actions can be either mental (*cetana*) or physical—corporeal and vocal acts (*kayika-* and *vacika-karma*). They are also divided into manifest acts (*vijñapti*) and unmanifested ones—*avijñapti*. The latter are, for our habits of thought, not acts, but their results, they are not physical, but moral. If a novice has taken the vows he has committed a physical, vocal action, which is *vijñapti*, but the lasting result is some moral excellence hidden in consciousness, and this is *avijñapti*. It constitutes a link between the act, and its future retribution; it is, therefore, the same as *samskara, apurva, adrsta* of the Brahmanical systems. Although by no means physical, since it lacks the general characteristic of matter which is impenetrability (*sapratighatva*), it nevertheless is brought by the Sarvastivadins (not by others) under the head of *rupa*, because of its close connexion with the physical act upon which it follows as a shadow cast from an object always follows that object.

B. CONSCIOUSNESS, PURE, WITHOUT CONTENT (CITTA=MANAS =VIJNANA).

1. *manas*, consciousness in the role of an independent, sixth, perceptive faculty, cognizing the non-sensuous, or abstract, objects (*dharmah*): it represents the preceding moment with regard to the *mano-vijnana*.

2. *Caksur-vijñana*, the same pure consciousness when associated with the visual sense.

3. *crotra-vijñana*, the same pure consciousness when associated with the auditory sense.

4. *ghrana-vijñana*, the same pure consciousness when associated with the olfactory sense.

5. *jihva-vijñana*, the same pure consciousness when associated with the taste sense.

6. *kaya-vijñana*, the same pure consciousness when associated with the tactile sense.

7. *mano-vijñana*, the same pure consciousness when associated with a previous moment of the same run of consciousness without participation of any of the five senses.

C. THE FORTY-SIX MENTAL ELEMENTS (CAITTA-DHARMA) OR FACULTIES INTIMATELY COMBINING WITH THE ELEMENT OF CONSCIOUSNESS (CITTA-SAMPRAYUKTA-SAMSKARA).

They are divided into—

1. 10 *citta-mahabhumika-dharma*, Mental Faculties.

2. 10 *kucala-mahabhumika-dharma*
3. 6 *kleca-mahabhumika-dharma*
4. 1 *akucala-mahabhumika-dharma*   Moral Forces
5. 10 *upakleca (paritta-) bhumika-dharma*
6. 8 *aniyata-bhumika-dharma*

Together 46.

A. *Ten General Mental Faculties present in every moment of Consciousness (citta-mahabhumika)—*

1. *vedana*   faculty of feeling (pleasant, unpleasant, indifferent).
2. *sanjna*   „   concepts (capable of coalescing with a word).
3. *cetana*   „   will, conscious effort (*citta-abhisamskara, citta-praspanda*).
4. *sparca*   „   sensation (comparable to a first "contact" between object, sense-organ, and consciousness).
5. *chanda*   faculty of desire (*abhiprete vastuny abhilasa*).
6. *prajna*   „   understanding, discriminating (*yena-
   (=*mati*)   sankirna iva dharmah puspanwa praviciyante*).
7. *smrti*   „   memory (*cetaso 'pramosah*).
8. *manasikara*   „   attention.
9. *adhimoksa*   „   inclination (*alambanasya gunato 'vadharanam*).
10. *samadhi*   „   concentration (*yena cittam prabandhena ekatralambane vartate*).

B. *Ten Universally "good" Moral Forces, present in every favourable moment of Consciousness (kucala-mahabhumika)—*

1. *craddha*   faculty of belief in retribution, the purity of mind, the reverse of passion (*cittasya prasadah*).
2. *virya*   „   courage in good actions (*kucala-kriyayam cetaso 'tyutsahah*).
3. *upeksa*   .   equanimity, indifference (*cittasya samata, yad-yogat cittam anabhogam vartate*).
4. *hri*   „   shyness, modesty, humility, being ashamed with reference to oneself. (*gauravam*). The reverse of IV, I.
5. *apatrapa*   „   aversion to things objectionable, feeling disgust with reference to other peoples' objectionable actions (*avadye bhayadarcita*). The reverse of IV, 2.
6. *alobha*   „   absence of love.

7. *advesa*   **faculty of absence of hatred.**

8. *ahimsa*   „   causing no injury.

9. *pras(c)rabdhi*   „   mental dexterity (*cittasya karmanyata, cittasya laghavam*).

10. *apramada*   „   acquiring and preserving good qualities (*kucalanam dharmanam pratilambha-nisevanam*).

C. *Six Universally "Obscured" Elements present in every unfavourable moment of Consciousness* (*kleca-maha-bhumika*)—

1. *moha* (=avidya)   faculty of ignorance, the reverse of *prayna* (I, 6), and therefore the primordial cause of the commotion (*duhkha*) of the world-process.

2. *pramada*   faculty of carelessness, the reverse of *apramade*, II, 10.

3. *kausidya*   „   mental heaviness, clumsiness, the reverse of *prasrabdhi*, II, 9.

4. *acraddha*   „   disturbed mind, the reverse of *craddha*, II, 1.

5. *styana*   „   sloth, indolence, inactive temperament.

6. *auddhatya*   „   being addicted to pleasure and sports, sanguine temperament (*cetaso' nupa-camah, nrtya-gitadi-crngara-vecya-al-amkara - kayauddhatya - sannicraya-dana-karmakah caitasika dharmah*).

These six faculties are not always absolutely bad; they sometimes may be indifferent (*avyakrta*) for the progress towards Final Deliverance, but they are nevertheless always "obscured" (*nivrta=achadita=klista*) by promoting the belief in an existing personality (*satkaya-anugraha-drsti-samprayhkta*). Always bad (*akucalav eva*) are the following two—

D. *Two Universally "bad" Elements present in every unfavourable moment of Consciousness* (*akucala-maha-bhumika-dharma*)—

1. *ahrikya*   **faculty of irreverence** (*agauravam=apraticala,*[12] *yad-yogad gunesu gunavatsu ca pud-*

----

[12] *pratica=guru-sthaniya.*

galesu gauravam na karoti), arroga-
gance, want of humility (abhaya-
vaca-vartita). The reverse of II, 4
(gaurava-pratidvandvo dharmah).

2. anapatrapya   „   not feeling indignant at offences done
by others (avadye sadbhir garhite
bhaya-a-darcitvam). The reverse of
II, 5.

E. · Ten vicious Elements of limited occurrence (upakleca
(paritta-) bhumika-dharma)—

1. krodha   faculty of anger, violence (vyapada-vihimsa-var-
jitah sattvasattvayor aghatah).

2. marksa   „   hypocrisy, deceit (of courtiers and
others).

3. matsarya   „   envy.

4. irsya   „   jealousy.

5. pradasa   „   approving objectionable things (savadya-
vastu-paramarca).

6. vihimsa   „   causing harm, menacing.

7. upanaha   „   breaking friendship.

8. maya   „   deceit.

9. catya   „   perfidy, trickery.

10. mada   „   complacency, self-admiration (cf. mana,
VI, 7).

These ten elements are described as purely mental (mano-
bhumika eva)-; they are never associated with any of the five
varieties of sensuous consciousness (na panca-vijnana-kayikah)
they cannot combine with the four alternating klecas (raga,
dvesa, mana, vicikitsa), but with moha=avidya alone, the
purely mental kleca. They must be suppressed by knowledge
(drsti-heya), not by concentration (bhavana-heya.) For all
these reasons they are classified as vices of a limited scope
(paritta-bhumika).

F. Eight Elements not having any definite place in the above
system, but capable of entering into various combinations.
(aniyata-bhumi-dharma)—

1. kaukrtya   faculty of repenting.

   middha   „   absent-mindedness, dreamy state of
   (=nidra)   mind.

3. vitarka   „   a searching state of mind.

4. vicara   „   a fixing state of mind.

5. *raga*   „   love, passion.
6. *dvesa*   „   hatred.
7. *mana*   „   pride, an exaggerated opinion of one's
                       own pre-eminence by real or imagi-
                       ned qualifications (cf. *mada,* V. 10).
8. *vicikitsa*   „   a doubting turn of mind.

Kaukrtya is brought under this head because it neither
has a place among the universal faculties, nor has it a definitely "good" or definitely "bad" significance: it can mean
repentance for a mad deed and being sorry for having e.g.
overdone in charity.

Middha can also have various moral aspects.

Vitarka and *vicara* are universal only on the *kama-Dhatu*.

Raga, dvesa, mana, and *vicikitsa* are four *klecas,* the fifth
being *moha* placed in III, 1. *Moha* is a universal "defiler",
entering in every unfavourable conscious moment, but the
other four "defilers" cannot combine with one another: if
there is *raga* associated with one's consciousness, there can be
no association with *dvesa* at the same time. Thus it is that
in every favourable, "good" moment, consciousness is associated with at least twenty-two elements: the ten universal ones
(I, 1-10), the ten universally good ones, and *vitarka, vicara*
(VI, 4-5). If repentance (VI, 1) is added, the number will
increase by one. In every unfavourable or "bad" moment the
minimum number will be twenty elements: the ten universal
ones (I, 1-10), the six universally "obscured" (III, 1-6), the two
universally bad (IV, 1-2), and *vitarka, vicara* (VI, 4-5). If all
the *samskrta-laksanas, citta* itself, its *lakshmanas* and *up-
alaksanas* are taken into account, the number will increase
accordingly (cf. p. 26, n. 2). Vasubandhu remarks that it is
very difficult to distinguish all these elements even in the long
run, let alone in a moment, but difficult does not mean impossible. Contradictory elements, as e.g., pleasure and pain,
cannot enter into the same combination, but contradiction is
often only on the surface, e.g. *styana* and *auddhatya,* an
inactive and an exuberant element, are present in every vicious
moment, it is some indulging in vice and some active participation. Whether the individual or the conscious state shall
be more passive or more active depends on the occasional predominance of one element over the others. In every moment,
or mental state, there always is one predominant element, just

as in material substances we have earth, water, fire and air,
according to the predominance of one of the *mahabhutas*
(cf. p. 11). Among the universally good elements indifference
(*upeksha* II, 3) and inclination (*adhimoksa,* II, 9) are not
contradictory: they are directed towards different objects:
indifference towards pain and pleasure, and inclination towards good deeds, they can go together. But *apramada*
(III, 2) are the reverse of one another, not mutual absence
alone, and therefore they never can combine.

Vitarka, Vicara

Vitarka and *vicara* are sub-conscious operations of the mind
(*na niccaya-dharmau*). *Vitarka* is "an indistinct murmur of
the mind", (*mano-jalpa*), which is searching (*paryesaka*) after
its object. In this initial stage (*anatyuha-avasthayam*), it is
simply a move of will (*cetana-vicesa*): when emerging into the
conscious plane (*atyuha-avasthayam*), it becomes a certain
thought (*prajna-vicesa*). *Vicara* is also an "indistinct murmur
of the mind", but it is attempting to fix (*pratyaveksaka*) its
object; it has the same two stages; it is also characterized as a
refinement (*suksmata*) of the coarser (*audarika*) *vitarka*. Since
both these functions are associated with sense-consciousness,
they very nearly approach the Kantian doctrine of synthesis of
apprehension preceded by the mind running through a variety
of sense-impressions, as far as they are sub-conscious operations
of the mind preceding a definite sense perception. The
Vaibhasikas maintain that there is some *vitarka* (=*vikalpa*) in
every moment of consciousness; they then call it *svabhava-
vikalpa;* but Vasubandhu seems to admit "pure sensation"
(reine Sinnlichkeit) without any participation of discursive
thought (*vikalpa*). Cf. Ab. K., i, 30; ii, 33. *Vyasa bhasya* in
i, 44, according to Professor B. Seal (*Positive Sciences*, p. 18),
trans, pure intuition (*nirvicara-nirvikalpa-prajna*) and "empirical" intuition (*sovichara-nirvikalpa-prajna*); the latter contains the three relations of Space, Time, and Causation, in
addition to pure consciousness.

D. FORCES WHICH CAN NEITHER BE INCLUDED AMONG MATERIAL
   NOR AMONG SPIRITUAL ELEMENTS (RUPA-CITTA-VIPRAYUKTA-
   SAMSKARA).

1. *prapti*   ...   a force which controls the collection of
                       the elements in an individual stream
                       of life (*santana*).

2. *aprapti* ... a force which occasionally keeps some elements in abeyance in an individual *santana*.

3. *nikaya-sabhagata* ... a force producing generality or homogeneity of existences, the counterpart of the realistic generality of the *Vaicesikas*.

4. *asanjnika* ... a force which (automatically, as a result of former deeds), transfers an individual into the realms of unconscious trance.

5. *asanjni-samapatti* ... a force stopping consciousness and producing the unconscious trance (through an effort).

6. *nirodha-samupatti* ... a force stopping consciousness and producing the highest, semi-conscious, dreamy trance.

7. *jivita* ... the force of life-duration, a force which at the time of birth forecasts the moment of death, just as the force with which an arrow is discharged forecasts the moment when it will fall down.

8. *jati* ... origination.
9. *sthiti* ... subsistence   the four *samskrta-laksa-*
10. *jara* ... decay   *nas*, cf. p. 33 above.
11. *anityate* ... extinction

12. *nama-kaya* ... the force imparting significance to words.

13. *Pada-kaya* the force imparting significance to sentences.

14. *vyanjana-kaya* the force imparting significance to articulate sounds.

E. IMMUTABLE ELEMENTS (ASAMSKRTA-DHARMA).

1. *akaca* ... space (empty).

2. *pratisankhya-nirodha* ... the supression of the manifestations of an element (*dharma*) through the

	action of understanding (*prajna*), as *e.g.* after having realized that the existence of a personality is an illusion a kind of eternal blank is substituted for this wrong idea.
3. *apratisankhya-* *-nirodha* ...	the same cessation produced not through knowledge, but in a natural way, through the extinction of the causes that produced a manifestation, as *e.g.* the extinction of the fire when there is no more fuel.

F. CASUAL INTERCONNEXION OF ELEMENTS (HETU-PRATYAYA)

4 *Pratyaya.*	6 *Hetu.*	5 *Phala.*
	1 *sahabhu-hetu*	. *purusakara-*
	2. *samprayukta-hetu.*	*phala.*
1. *hetu-pratyaya.*	3. *sabhaga-hetu*	2. *nisyanda-*
	4. *sarvatraga-hetu.*	*phala.*
	5. *vipaka-hetu.*	3. *vipaka-phala.*
2. *samanantara-pratyaya.*		
3. *alambana-pratyaya.*		
4. *adhipati-pratyaya.*	6. *karana-hetu.*	4. *adhipati-phala.*
		5. *visamyoga-phala.*

As to the meaning, *Samanantara-pratyaya* (=*upasarpana-pratyaya*) is similar to the *samavayi-karana* of the *Vaicesikas*. *Alambana*, cf. p. 50, note. *Adhipati-pratyaya* and *karana hetu* are similar to the *karana* (=*sadhakatamam karanam*) of the *Vaicesikas*. *Visamyoga-phala is nirvana*. (See pp. 25-26).

G. THE TWELVE CONSECUTIVE STAGES IN THE EVER-REVOLVING LIFE-PROCESS.

(*Avastthika* or *prakaraika pratitya-samutpada*)

    I.   *Former Life*

1. *avidya*	...	delusion (*caitta-dharma*, III, 1).
2. *samskara*	...	(=*karma*).

    II.   *Present Life*

3. *vijnana*	...	first moment of a new life, the moment of conception (=*pratisandhi-vijnana*).

4. *nama-rupa*	...	the five *skandhas* in the embryo before the formation of the sense-organs.
5. *sad-ayatana*	...	the formation of the organs.
6. *sparca*	...	organs and consciousness begin to co-operate.
7. *vedana*	...	definite sensations.
8. *trsna*	...	awakening of the sexual instinct, beginning of new *karma*.
9. *upadana*	...	various pursuits in life.
0. *bhava*	...	life, *i.e.* various conscious activities (=*karma-bhava*).

III. *Future Life*

11. *jati*	...	rebirth.
12. *jara-marana*	...	new life, decay, and death.

The five *skandhas* are present during the whole process; the different stages receive their names from the predominant *dharma* (cf. p. 24, n. 86). The first two stages indicate the origin of the life-process (*duhkha-samudaya*).

In regard to a future life Nos. 8-10 perform the same function as Nos. 1-2 in regard to the present life. Therefore the series represents an ever revolving "wheel"

The End

INDEX

I. Proper Names

Vya 37, 38, 29, *passim.*
Yocomitra, 2, 3, 4, 18, *passim.*

Yoga, 37, 38.

II. SANSKRIT TERMS

(The Sanskrit Terms and their explanations are to be found on pp. 80-93).

7.